FIRST AID MWE

What Everyone Needs To Know About Healing The Mind, Will, And Emotion

Written By Sammy Vale

Freedom House Publishing 2015

Table of Contents

Introduction

A Brief Lesson From History

"History doesn't repeat itself, but it does rhyme." — Mark Twain

The present state of our inner being, our mind, will, and emotion, rhymes with the history of our outer being. To understand our present, take a look at our past. Consider how intangible the concept of germs would have been to the world before we could see microorganisms with our eyes. Consider how intangible to you, is the realm of thought, inner will, and emotion. But what if we can listen to the rhyme and meter of history's repeating chorus and verse? What if, by means of poetic alignment, we could understand our present through the parable of our past? First Aid MWE is a leap forward in a culture that cannot see what ails them. Poetry and parable have long taught men to see the invisible.

"Since the fall of the Western Roman Empire, there have been three major bubonic plague epidemics, which afflicted large segments of the population in the continuous Eurasian landmass and North Africa. Death quickly followed the trade routes of the times. The death toll is almost incomprehensible. The Plague of Justinian (6th Century A.D.), the Black Death (14th Century A.D.), and the Bubonic Plague (1665-1666, which coincided with the Great Fire of London) caused an estimated 137 million dead in a world much more sparsely populated than it is today.

To make matters even worse, one must also remember that these pestilences assailed and ravaged mankind at a time when the average life span was short --- less than two decades during the Middle Ages. Survival to age five was a miracle not only because of endemic disease, dirt and filth, concomitant poor hygiene and sanitation, but also because of the primitive state of medical knowledge. Pestilential disease thrived under such conditions. Moreover, during the Middle Ages, bathing and cleanliness, even in the upper classes, was a rarity, being viewed as unhealthy as well as irreverent ---acts of vanity in the face of God."

It is incomprehensible to us, living in the age that we do, what it must have been like to live through a plague that was killing one of every three people you knew. The black death (bubonic plague) provided such odds throughout Europe.

Italian writer Giovanni Boccaccio lived through the plague as it ravaged the city of Florence in 1348. The experience inspired him to write The Decameron, a story of seven men and three women who escape the disease by fleeing the city. In his introduction to the fictional portion of his book, Boccaccio gives a graphic description of the effects of the epidemic on his city. Here are some selected portions of his account:

"The symptoms were not the same as in the East, where a gush of blood from the nose was the plain sign of inevitable death; but it began both in men and women with certain swellings in the groin or under the armpit. They grew to the size of a small apple or an egg, more or less, and were vulgarly called tumours. In a short space of time these tumours spread from the two parts named all over the body. Soon after this the symptoms changed and black or purple spots appeared on the arms or thighs or any other part of the body, sometimes a few large ones, sometimes many little ones. These spots were a certain sign of death, just as the original tumour had been and still remained."

Giovanni describes the sheer quantity of deaths, the scores of empty houses, and the lifestyles of many who were still alive. Living as through they were kindling desperately navigating through a forest fire of illness, many believed that even speaking of the ill might cause infection. It was this fear that caused them to live in a state of forced denial. All industry and production had halted and one could only survive by scavenging what was left behind. Taking possession of an empty house, the living would moderately drink whatever wine they might find (moderate only because vanity and excess were suspected causes of this bubonic "punishment"), feign merriness in a desperate attempt to outwit the plague, they would rest, and carry on trying not to touch anything that could be smoldering with the curse. When resources ran out they would move on to the next molted shell, scavenging whatever small bits of life were left in what was once a glad home.

"Such fear and fanciful notions took possession of the living that almost all of them adopted the same cruel policy, which was entirely to avoid the sick and everything belonging to them. By so doing, each one thought he would secure his own safety.

One citizen avoided another, hardly any neighbour troubled about others, relatives never or hardly ever visited each other. Moreover, such terror was struck into the hearts of men and women by this calamity, that brother abandoned brother, and the uncle his nephew, and the sister her brother, and very often the wife her husband. What is even worse and nearly incredible is that fathers and mothers refused to see and tend their children, as if they had not been theirs.

The plight of the lower and most of the middle classes was even more pitiful to behold. Most of them remained in their houses, either through poverty or in hopes of safety, and fell sick by thousands. Since they received no care and attention, almost all of them died. Many ended their lives in the streets both at night and during the day; and many others who died in their houses were only known to be dead because the neighbors smelled their decaying bodies. Dead bodies filled every corner. Most of them were treated in the same manner by the survivors, who were more concerned to get rid of their rotting bodies than moved by charity towards the dead. With the aid of porters, if they could get them, they carried the bodies out of the houses and laid them at the door; where every morning quantities of the dead might be seen. They then were laid on biers or, as these were often lacking, on tables."

Certainly the insanity of this incomprehensible terror is too much to grasp. It is even more incomprehensible to know that had the populace simply washed their hands and managed their sewage, this disease would not have reached a notable status. This fine detail, this simple discovery still undiscovered, can only be described by an ancient greek word, "hamartia."

Hamartia has a beautiful complexity expressed in simplicity. I feel it is best defined in these examples. A man begins a thousand mile journey which ends a thousand miles off course because of a one degree error in his initial direction. The one degree error was his hamartia. A space shuttle explodes moments after liftoff because an engineer failed to carry a one in his complex calculations for the diameter of a moving part in the fuel thruster. The failure to notice the carryover was his hamartia. An archer falls to the arrow of his enemy because the arrow he fired first, missed its mark. This was due to a two inch misplacement of his foot. The misplacement of his foot was his hamartia. Hamartia is the smallest discoverable error which causes a greater tragedy.

Simple unknown sanitation habits were the hamartia of the Europeans living during the high middle ages. The Bible often crudely translates this word "hamartia" as "sin." So ironically, as the europeans suspected, 137 million deaths were in fact the punishment for their "sins." The "sin" of their unsanitary habits were the entirely common practices of normal people. A person with the sanitary habits of our day and age would likely have ended up in an insane asylum.

Today we live in a state of forced denial similar to that of those trying to survive the bubonic plague. Much like those survivors, or in many cases, future victims of the black death, we do not have the foundation or direction to find solutions. We merely live alongside the ill, avoiding them until we cannot. According to the National Institute of Mental Illness, one out of every five Americans has a diagnosable mental illness, not including addiction. Add addiction to those statistics and it raises the toll beyond black death numbers. Add to that sum the consideration that these numbers only reflect those brave enough or ruined enough to admit their problem. Many more of us suffer with our "lumps" hidden behind closed doors. Our minds are sick and we are too afraid to admit it because, like those who suffered through the bubonic plague, we have no accessible methods for dealing with it.

Our mental and emotional ailments have reached such catastrophic levels that they are now suspected to be the cause, or at least prime aggravators of many physical disorders including genetic ones. In other words, our epidemic of mental illness has had such profound impact that it is now bleeding over into physical manifestation and marking even our genes with its trauma. Most of us suffer with symptoms that, like many bubonic hosts propagating the disease, we are not willing to discuss with others. Instead we live alongside one another doing our best to imitate the norms. We try to suppress those behaviors which we recognize as destructive to our happiness, our relationships, and our consciences. Do we have a choice?

At this point your denial is kicking in. You are already trying to either dismiss yourself from fault or separate yourself from the audience of readers. But whether you are in perfect mental heath or simply in denial is no matter. Remember that the world's worst plagues were not caused by the afflicted. They were caused by a lack of sanitation in a growing populace whose culture had not yet developed their personal hygiene nor the common medical knowledge to a level capable of supporting their **population density**. This is, in nearly exact terms, the cause of our current collective mental health condition.

Essential Yet Obscured

Imagine for a moment that you are walking toward your work with a bleeding gash hidden under your jacket. You peek at it for the fifteenth time this morning. "It's not that bad," you say to yourself as you enter through the doors. You remind yourself of what the last person who saw your wound told you, "Just take it one day at a time." You say to yourself,

"Just get through another day at work and eventually this pain will go away." You've had your gash for a few days now and it did get a little better. It doesn't bleed as much now and the initial sting has faded, but God help you if someone bumps into the wound again.

You wish you could just tell everyone to stop bumping into you. You wish you could show them your huge bleeding gash so they would realize how horrible it is for you when they bump into it. Then again, how much worse would it be to have all of them looking at your wound? There would be that "glad it's not me" pity and the useless clichés, and then the stunned people who would avoid you altogether because you are too fragile. People so rarely offer any real solutions. "No, I can make it through another day with this. It will eventually go away...I hope."

Oh, I forgot to mention, there's no such thing as First Aid in this imaginary world. It's not hard to imagine how infection and illness would thrive, mostly because we have a written history of medicine and hygiene for the last few thousand years. We know what the world looks like without proper medical and hygienic knowledge. Let it sink in then, that we still live in an age where First Aid for our minds is so obscure that even now you are among one of the smallest people groups on the planet who have heard of it. This is not something that can stay small or obscure. Humanity is right on the brink of a renaissance of consciousness.

We tend to think that in one hundred years or so people will look back and scoff at our technology or how little we knew about what lies beyond our own solar system. That is because those are the things we are currently focused on as a society. It is so much more likely that the things we are ignoring will be revealed by time as our greatest flaws.

We can see the evolution of our minds and our cultures laid out right in front of us. We can see where we have been and where we are going as a species. In the next few hundred years, humanity will thrive as children with more favorable characteristics for survival and regeneration begin to dominate the populace. With the evolution of a global society, empathy and advanced social and emotional skills will make or break the coming generations. Those with stronger, more resilient minds and greater empathy will survive those without. It's time that we all learn basic First Aid skills for our minds, our inner will, and our emotions.

By now you have figured out that the wound you were hiding under your jacket was not physical, but emotional. I hesitated to use the word emotion, because we have a culture that tends to dismiss all things emotional as secondary or altogether unimportant. We couldn't be more wrong. In fact, evidence about the human limbic and endocrine systems show that information travels in both directions between our body and mind. In other words, physical changes in the body can affect our emotions. Perhaps more importantly, emotions triggered by our thought life can have a profound effect on our body. So even if one were to insist that emotional health is secondary to physical health, they should know that having a healthy mind is a huge part of having a healthy body.

This guide will offer conversational sequences and mental stimulations aimed at treating common mental and emotional injuries. Through study, practice and experience you will have the essential knowledge of First Aid for the mental and emotional health of those around you and for yourself as well.

First Aid Culture

I want you to read an excerpt from an article written about First Aid in Nigeria. Nigeria is one of a handful of countries where First Aid is simply not part of the culture. It is in a cultural blind spot much like the way mental and emotional well being is for most western nations.

"Also, for a 29 years old fitness centre administrative assistant, Funke Lanre, having knowledge of first aid is thought to be exclusively for health professionals. "I thought only health professionals like nurses and doctors can administer first aid to people especially during accidents and

other health emergencies. Though my organization has a first aid box at the reception, it is controlled by the physiotherapist working with our customers. No other staff has been taught how to use it. The only thing I know is that there are paracetamol tablets in the first aid pack. I can't conveniently say I know about other tools in the pack," she added.

Lanre gave a scenario in which she and some passengers were involved in motor accidents but none could get first aid from other motorists until they all went to a nearby hospital, which ideally should be the second line of action after administering first aid to accident victims. "When the bus I was traveling in had an accident, we resorted to self help even when there where other motorists plying the road, none could come down to assist us. Some passengers were profusely bleeding until we all went to a nearby hospital to treat ourselves," she added." (Martins Ifijeh- 'Embracing First Aid Culture-This Day Live- Written Jun. 2015)

You and I can look at this scenario and see the absurdity of this problem. We wonder, "How can entire bus of people look at each other's bleeding wounds, walk past a highway full of people in cars, and not one has the tools to help the other?" Yet this is exactly how many of us experience the mental and emotional wounds we often see in ourselves and the people around us. We are helpless, fearful, and overly dependent on professional help which we usually cannot afford. It is time to change our culture by first changing our mindset.

The thing that makes First Aid for the mind, will, and emotion beautiful is also what makes it elusive. The tools we use are intangible. Their beauty is that they cannot be misplaced or ruined. They can be freely copied and multiplied without production. Their elusiveness is that they are every bit as useful as a physical tool, and yet you cannot see or touch them. As simple minded as it sounds, many will fail to grasp them for that reason alone. Why do you think pills are so popular? We tend to feel more comfortable with the tangible. Yet the solution, like our problem, is not often something we can hold in our hands.

So with these things in mind, let me share a short description of what a First Aid culture looks like and believes.

- A responsible adult knows how to help others.

- A general belief is shared that "Me doing my best is better than nobody doing anything".

- Many issues are treated at home without a doctor.

- Injury is common. Tools exist to treat injury, so everyone becomes competent in using them.

- By having the tools and knowledge to respond quickly, I can prevent further issues and even prevent tragedy.

If you didn't notice, let me point out that the list above works for First Aid in general, body or mind. In regard to bleeding, breathing, and hearts beating, we have no problem agreeing that we all have a responsibility to respond with our best efforts and knowledge. Yet the idea that I can help treat trauma, fear, and depression tends to garner trepidation followed by a metaphoric "washing of the hands." Suddenly we are all like Nigerian motorists facing a crowd of gushing wounds. Made useless by our lack of knowledge, we become nothing more than a stream of gawkers driving past our friends and loved ones on the highway of life.

This alone should wake us up to the fact that as a society we have failed to see the importance of MWE health. To bring this point even further, it is important to note that in the case of injury to a person's mind, will, or emotion it is entirely common that this person, if untreated, will go on to cause similar injury to other people around them. The abused often go on to become abusers. Children with parents who suffer from depression are more likely to also become depressed, and the list could go on. The fact is, just like physical injuries, the faster we can address MWE issues, less complications can arise. We also see fewer long term effects, less "infection" (degradation of personality), and less "scarring" (deformation of character). The sooner we can catch an issue, the less likely it is to become something that only a clinician can treat. It is time we become as familiar with basic MWE issues as we are with basic medical issues.

In this guide you will not find twelve steps on dealing with addiction. You will not find tips for dealing with insomnia, phobias, or depression. Like most plagues, these ailments are the fruit of a deeper problem. Also, as in most plagues, these deeper problems actually have simpler solutions. Getting treatment for surface issues is important, but in this guide we want to deal with root issues rather than stay in a nonstop cycle of managing symptoms. We have found from experience that once the root issues are dealt with, the symptoms we tend to over analyze start to disappear.

MWE

Let's start with the basics. I'm sure you've figured out that MWE stands for mind, will, and emotion.

- **The Mind** refers to the individual thought life. If I were looking at a scan of your brain activity, the areas that show activity would tell me what is on your "mind." Issues of the mind are thought issues that cause pain, suffering, and destructive behaviors. Most of our First Aid procedures will occur here.

- **The Will** refers to something a bit harder to grasp. It is not the content of the thoughts but the patterns, associations, and unseen driving force that activates thought. If I were looking at a scan of your brain activity, the order in which things light up and the patterns with which activity moves through the brain would indicate to me your will. The will refers to what you want and thus drives the direction of your thoughts. The core of human will is an elusive thing to study. It always ends in the philosophical realm because we must eventually ask, "What is

14

consciousness?" I won't try to answer that for you. We must simply accept that we are alive and thus *life* is the mechanism that fuels our will. Regardless of how convoluted our logic may become, the driving force behind all thought is life. That logic may express life through selfishness when the scope and focus remains on self. That logic may express life in destruction when the individual has judged others to be detrimental to life. That logic may express life in self destruction when the individual believes that they are detrimental to the living. But when our logic lines up with the will of life itself, our thoughts become clear, our lives become more purposeful, and our experiences become saturated with meaning.

- **Emotion** refers to your state of mind as a response to thought. We all know what it means to have a "feeling", yet understanding our feelings is much more difficult. Emotion is a cyclical system; a blend of will driving thought, thought activating glands, and glands releasing chemicals which then affect the will. Emotion, often disregarded as less important than cognition, is actually more powerful and more important to our overall health and well being. If you aim to be effective at First Aid MWE, you will start to pay closer attention to emotions.

Empowerment

Surgeons are specialists with a specific skill set to fix complex problems in high risk situations. If your ankle were shattered a surgeon could put it back together. Can a surgeon splint a broken ankle? Sure. Do you need a surgeon to splint a broken ankle? No. Doctors are highly trained in a wide field of medical expertise. If your ankle was swollen, turning black, and getting worse, a doctor could figure out the problem, help with pain management, and point you in the right direction. Can a doctor splint a broken ankle? Yes. Do you need a doctor to splint a broken ankle? No. Paramedics are trained, experienced experts in first response skills and first aid. Can a paramedic splint a broken ankle? Definitely. Do you need a paramedic to splint a broken ankle? Not if you already know how to do it. What happens if you splint the ankle and it gets worse?

15

That's when you know that the problem is more complicated than you originally detected and it's time to move up the ladder of health practitioners in search of meeting a more specific need.

Psychiatrists, Psychologists, Counselors, Social Workers, and Peer Specialists form a similar ladder. But what they cannot do is be everywhere. They cannot be in the moment with you. They cannot have the profound and lasting impact of an organic social relationship like your personal friends and family.

For your friends, your family, and yourself, you are the first line of defense and will be the first to recognize an issue while it is still not a big deal. If you are the kind of person who prefers to keep things not a big deal, then I suggest you learn these tools inside and out and treat your issues swiftly rather than letting them fester.

I will be the first to tell you that First Aid MWE will be new for many of you. Some of it may seem strange, but just imagine the first audience to learn CPR. "You want us to put our mouths on their mouths and our hands on their chest?" Trust me, this won't be nearly that strange or awkward. Much of it can be done through conversation or through a simple exercise focusing on a memory. People talk about their pain for a reason. We can be more than just another gawker.

This manual is full of actionable steps that you can lead yourself and others through. Carefully take your time with each step. Quickly reading through a list of steps without engaging will do absolutely nothing for you. That would be equivalent to reading a first aid manual without ever touching a wound. Be prepared to get real.

Essential Knowledge

H.E.L.P

There are many wonderful reasons to want to learn First Aid MWE and practice it right away. I want to encourage you to do just that. Before we start, I want you to recall your airline flight attendant's instructions on how to use the oxygen mask. "First, take your mask and place it over your own mouth and nose. You're no good to the rest of us unconscious. THEN reach over and help anyone near you who may need assistance." The same is true in First Aid MWE. Many times in an effort to ignore or deny our own pain, we want to become rescuers. Being a rescuer as a form of denial will always project the wrong attitude and will hurt more than it will help. This kind of "help," will not help. Start helping others by first walking yourself through the healing tools in this book.

H is for Humility

If we make First Aid MWE about our own ego, we will use it to trick ourselves into feeling powerful by making someone else feel like a victim. Even though we are not the victimizers, we must be aware that a desire to juxtapose our benevolence with the emotional poverty of another is all too often the hidden psychology behind giving.

As you progress through these tools, you will likely realize that you have a few wounds, pains, and burns that need attention. Unlike the body, the mind does not heal autonomously. It can only heal once the memories have been accessed and understood. Pay attention to the memories that surface as you read. They will likely be your first and most important places in need of first aid.

Stepping into this world you are going to humbly take a good look at yourself and admit that you will never be graceful enough to be above falling down and scraping your knee. We all need first aid at times, and we all get sick sometimes. It's not that some of us are better than others, rather we each get exposed to different dangers. We all need help. You happen to have come to a place where you know it and you are learning what to do about it. Being helpful toward others requires humility toward yourself.

E is for Empowerment

The culture of First Aid MWE is one of empowerment. Having the power to find resolution for our own internal issues is a basic right and ought to be a common passage into the self-reliance of adulthood. In the same spirit, we help others because we want them to be powerful and free from their own pain, anxiety, and debilitating thoughts.

Becoming a powerful person means you control you and I control me and we both take full responsibility for that fact. Once we grab hold of this concept, we begin to realize that it is a lie to say "You made me angry." The truth is, you can't make me anything. I made me angry. Thinking this way will help you to clarify boundaries that get fuzzy when you give and receive help. A healthy approach looks like this: I am a friend. I have tools that have helped me and some other people. I can show them to you if you like, but I am not signing up to be responsible for your thought life.

If I offered you some hydrogen peroxide and a band-aid to put on your cut and then you called me the next week to complain that the cut was now infected, I would very politely tell you that it is not my problem. If at this point I still want to offer some help, I may ask you some good questions to help you discover why the cut is infected which will hopefully help you to keep it clean until it heals. I cannot empower anyone by becoming their band-aid nurse nor will you empower anyone in MWE care if you become their emotional rescuer. Being helpful means we empower others to be responsible for themselves.

L is for Learning

You will always be learning. In MWE care, there are no masters, no gurus, and no lone rangers. We are all students. We are all practicing. We are all different people, thus each person's issues will require something unique. First Aid MWE is a collection of tools developed by people from different walks of life, from different continents, and with different ideas about treatment. However, one thing is common in every tool as well as every person who brought something to the table: none are the be-all and end-all. As first aid practitioners, we share our knowledge, our pain, our failures, fears, and secrets. We do it because in doing so, we learn more about ourselves, each other, humanity, and life.

In a learning culture we get into the habit of asking questions. Most of our First Aid tools are nothing more than really good questions. We don't think of truth as relative. Nor do we expect that every person will understand and express truth through the same lenses or voice. To be effective in navigating the mind, will, and emotion of another person you must leave yourself at the door and remember that others are not you. They are not like you. They don't think, see, or feel the same as you, and they don't need to become you. Being helpful means remembering that you are always learning and always listening.

P is for Purity

For all of the previous reasons, it is important for anyone who wishes to treat the wounds of another person to do two things. First, allow someone else to treat some of your wounds. The experience will be invaluable. Second, take a moment to mentally prepare yourself before using MWE tools. Do this the same way you might wash your hands before bandaging a cut.

Not one human being is invincible; every one of us has real issues. Having issues to deal with doesn't disqualify you from helping others. Being unwilling to admit and/or deal with those issues, does. It means

19

that you're not ready, and that's okay. However if you are ready to be open and honest with someone about your stuff, that's called humility, but humility alone does not purify our intentions.

No one has perfect relationships, no one. We all have work to do in defining and in **fine tuning** our relationships. Having relationship issues doesn't disqualify you from helping others. However, being unwilling to let others be powerful or, conversely, being unwilling to be assertive, could infect the wounds you are trying to heal. MWE culture is about empowerment, but simply being a "powerful person" does not purify your intentions.

Life is a grand mystery which none have solved. We each carry a unique knowledge, experience, and perspective. Having limited knowledge does not disqualify you from helping others. However, if you do ever come to believe that you have nothing left to learn, then you are immediately disqualified. MWE culture is about learning. The one who remains a student will constantly improve, but this alone cannot purify your intentions.

Ultimately, we conclude that our culture is about imperfect people helping imperfect people with their imperfections. It's the quintessential human experience. Love. It means I choose to be good to you. You make the choice to be good to someone and you hold yourself responsible for that choice. You neither glorify their issues nor demonize them; in doing so you can see them clearly and help them effectively. When we come as humble students with powerful tools and genuine compassion, we epitomize MWE care. I recognize this final and comprehensive value as purity. Being helpful means embracing the purity of, "I choose to be good to you."

First Aid MWE Culture is about **HELP**:

- **H**umility

- **E**mpowerment

- **L**earning

- **P**urity

In order to be helpful we want to be full of HELP. Full of humility: knowing that we are in all ways equal with those we help. Full of an empowering attitude: having neither controlling interest nor obligation to help. Full of teachability: coming as one who seeks to learn rather than to show off. Full of purity: letting go of all intentions except the singular intention to do good for the benefit of a fellow person.

Heart Wash

To be "HELP-Full" we intentionally empty ourselves of all other thoughts and desires and allow humility, empowerment, learning, and purity to fill those places. This brings us to our very first exercise, a heart wash.

To wash the heart you simply give yourself a moment to visualize an exchange. In your mind, you are holding out all of your selfish baggage. You release it. In it's place comes humility, empowerment, learning, and purity. In doing this you do the MWE equivalent of washing your hands before applying First Aid.

HERE ARE THE STEPS:

I *visualize myself holding out my heart.*

I look at it and notice if it seems dirty, wounded, or otherwise imperfect. If I am feeling troubled or negative, I say out loud what needs to be washed away.

"I need to wash away _____(frustration, selfishness, pride, etc.)_____."

I watch expectantly for something that represents purity to wash away everything I sensed and even the things I did not recognize. I usually see something like water or sometimes bright light or mist.

I watch quietly and patiently until I see or sense that my heart is clean.

Once I feel that anything selfish or negative has left, I invite the water to fill up every chamber and vein in my body. I let myself feel it. Once I can sense that the transaction is complete, I am in the right state of mind to be helpful.

Without this step, I risk causing possible infection by transferring my own issues or agenda into the situation.

This exercise may sound unusual or trite, but remember that just over one hundred years ago, so did actual hand washing. As humanity matures, these practices will become much more important. So pay attention, and you may as well get used to the fact that this will all sound new and strange. Once you do it proficiently, you will remember a time when this simple heart washing felt awkward, and perhaps you will have a loving laugh at yourself.

What Not To Do

Don't play doctor. There are much healthier ways to boost your confidence that won't hurt your friends and family. First Aid MWE is for the benefit of the person who was brave enough to be vulnerable. Don't help others for the sake of yourself; it makes no sense.

Don't give advice. The moment you give advice you become responsible for the outcome. Empower your friend to discover their own course of action. You will notice that First Aid MWE tools are all questions, not answers. If you think you have an answer, try to think of a good question instead.

Don't talk when you could be listening. The desire to talk at a friends pain rather than listen is often a symptom that you have a similar issue to work out. If this is the case, deal with your issue first and then tell your friend about it at another time.

Don't judge. Just because you don't understand the issue doesn't mean that it's not a real struggle for your friend. Be honoring and reverent. People don't have to be real with you, and if you respond with judgment or condescension, they never will again. Ever feel like the world is full of "fake people?" People are only "fake" when they don't know if they can trust your heart.

Don't look surprised. Surprise is often interpreted as judgment even when it's not. Surprise says to the other person, "I cannot identify with your problem." It's the wrong signal to send.

Be careful about nodding your head. You may be simply trying to show empathy or show that you are listening but you might be interpreted as saying "Yes" or "I agree with your logic," when you don't mean to.

Be careful about shaking your head too. We don't say "No" with our head for the same reasons we don't nod. It's ambiguous communication in a time when you need precise communication. If you want to give assurance or empathy, do it intentionally by using words. "I'm so sorry that happened," is much clearer than shaking your head "no."

Don't force solutions. You may think you know what they need when in fact, you don't. Yet even if you know with certainty what is causing the problem, the real issue is that it's not your journey. Therefore it's not your discovery to make. Even though your tools are mostly questions, when you feel certain about where those questions will lead you, your tone and directive will betray you. The bottom line is that you need to trust what comes from the person who is hurting.

Don't diagnose. Diagnoses are tools for clinicians to keep track of how they plan to treat their patients' issues. You are not a doctor helping a patient. You are a friend helping a friend. Diagnoses often serve no good purpose for hurting people. Diagnoses usually occlude a wider spectrum of issues in the same way a cowbell at high volume can occlude the symphony of music that accompanies it. Additionally, they often give capable people a crutch of excuses and give undue power to an issue that might have been a simple fix.

Don't take sides or give opinions. This is another form of judgment and should be avoided for the same reasons. If you are willing to judge the person your friend is speaking poorly of, this lets them know that you may also be willing to judge them when they are not around. You may unintentionally mark yourself as an unsafe person who cannot be trusted with the real issues.

Don't ever tell someone what's going on inside of them! It's highly offensive and inappropriate. Again, even if you're pretty certain; it's not your right to make that discovery. If you want to end a relationship, this is a pretty good way to do it. It might feel like a good way to speed things along, but MWE care is not about the destination. It's about the journey. There are literally no shortcuts.

Empowerment

You don't need to dwell on this list of "what not to do". Just keep in mind a few simple do's while in an MWE conversation.

- Stay Humble, Empowering, Teachable and Pure of Heart

- Smile and Listen, But Stay Neutral

- Use Mostly Questions

These are not hard-and-fast rules. Ultimately you are in charge of your own relationships. Every connection has its own unique and living nature. You're a good person and you care about the people around you; that's genuine, and that's enough. I offer these guidelines because they might help you to avoid common dangers and pitfalls. My hope is that by over preparing you for something that will eventually become natural, we will make smooth the learning phase where things still feel unnatural.

Now that you have caught the spirit and culture of First Aid MWE, you are in the right mindset to learn how it's done. In our next chapters, you will have a beautiful reference guide for dealing with specific issues. I encourage you to read and practice them each individually. These tools are only effective if you have them with you, but you don't have them just because you have the book. They must be pulled out of the book and put inside of you. The best way to accomplish that is to practice and experience them for yourself. As you read through this manual, immerse yourself in the tools and interact with the *promptings given in italics*.

PART 1

FLESH WOUNDS

ABCDEF PROGRESSION

Dealing With Flesh Wounds

So by now you are wondering what you actually do to apply First Aid MWE. Most MWE care is done in either conversation, a mental exercise, or both. This is a brief outline of how a First Aid MWE conversation will progress **when dealing with flesh wounds.** We call these issues flesh wounds because they deal with pain that was initially caused by an external force or circumstance. Remember the steps by their alphabetical order: A-B-C-D-E-F

A. **Awareness**- This is the moment you realize that there's an MWE problem. You realize that someone needs first aid.

B. **Bruises/Burns/Bleeding**- You ask good questions to identify what you are dealing with. The wounds we will talk about in Part 1 all start with the letter "B": Bruising, Burns, and Bleeding.

C. **C (See) the memory**- The goal here is to inspect the wound. MWE wounds happen in the thought life. So in this step, we establish a way to examine those thoughts and memories by seeing them.

D. **Detoxify**- This is where we clean up the wound by asking up to five simple questions.

E. **Exchange**- Once we wash out the toxic thoughts, we exchange them with thoughts that will protect us from another infection. These "antibacterial thoughts" are easy to find and fun to use.

F. **Follow-through**- Finally, we bandage the wound by protecting it with a plan for how to respond in the future.

A

AWARE

Aware

Have you ever been in a conversation with someone and realized that things just got real? They are now expressing real pain, fear, or confusion. Often, that scares us, but it doesn't have to. Usually there's that moment of controlled internal panic where you're scrambling for something to equalize the pressure in the room. Suddenly, your mind is sorting through all those Dr. Phil clichés that seem to make everything better, at least momentarily. When you can't think of any good clichés, you start thinking of sentences that start with "Well, at least...", hoping that there's a simple silver lining that will make the pain worthwhile. It's in these moments that you are in a First Aid MWE situation, and you will finally know exactly what to do.

Aware of Personality as a Body

To better understand the concept of MWE injury, let's take a closer look at the analogy of the human personality as a body.

The skin represents our social personality. Although skin is sensitive and vulnerable, it serves as a protective layer for the inner workings of the person. Without it, the inner person and their parts would be completely vulnerable and eventually cease to function.

29

Tissues and organs represent the many parts and functions of our emotional personality. These are parts of us that work on a tangible level while remaining "under the surface" of our personality. We are aware of them as one might be aware of their heart rate, stomach, and muscles. I would describe this awareness as my inner voice.

Finally reaching the deepest interior of our person, we find bones and marrow. The marrow represents our inner will, and the hardened bone surrounding it is our resolve to protect and animate that will. These are the very core needs and instincts which make us human. These deep drives inside of us include both instinctual, almost animal like needs, along with the personal and existential needs for love, connection, serenity, and happiness. This, I believe, is the foundation for a more complete picture of our true personality. Like marrow, these core needs don't just drive us, they create a DNA of identity. They make us...us.

The type of MWE injury and the depth of its trauma will determine how you respond to it. Social injury, for instance, may do damage to your reputation, but this kind of injury is only "skin deep". Though it can temporarily stun you, it is unlikely to incapacitate you. On the other hand, a severe blow to your identity, like a broken bone, can and will likely disable you for a longer period of time. Your first response to injury can prevent a great deal of pain or additional injury. With this greater understanding in mind, let's look through a list of common wounds and better understand how to recognize them in the future.

Aware of Wounded Words

Wounds are defined as an injury caused by an outside source which penetrates or otherwise damages the skin (protective layer). We use the word "wound" to describe the feeling of our internal person being violated. Sometimes we are more specific: "That cut me deep." "I was completely burned by the incident." "His ego was badly bruised." "I don't know what to do; I am broken."

We intuitively understand the concept of an MWE wound because, metaphorically speaking, our inner man is built the same as our outer man. Pain or disfunction are the telltale signs of any injury whether in the mind or body. Our empathy should become alert when we hear these kinds of descriptive injury phrases.

Aware of Anxiety

Have you ever nursed a painful injury? Have you noticed how it seems that everyone and everything is trying to bump into it? You walk into a crowd and your whole body goes into a state of tense readiness. This is not dissimilar to the way we feel when our inner man is hurting and we are about to walk into a family gathering, school, or work. That uneasy feeling is telling you about a wound serious enough that it requires your attention. When you or someone you know seems to be in this state, it should alert you to the fact that first aid may be needed.

Aware of Offenses

Who is that one person who immediately puts you in a state of stress? You feel yourself tense up when you hear their name, or when you see their face. You feel stress when you hear or imagine their voice. Your mind is telling you about a wound. We want to deal with this kind of wounding quickly and repeatedly in order to prevent infection and bitterness.

Aware of Triggers

You know how certain situations just drive you crazy? Hmm... maybe not. Often times this one is much easier to spot in someone else. Do you have a friend, spouse, or child who blows up or shuts down every time... (fill in the blank) happens?

For me, it was anytime I felt accused. As the youngest child of four, I was an easy scapegoat growing up. I have an impressive collection of memories involving me getting into trouble for crimes I did not commit. Well, to be honest, some were just crimes I did not commit alone. Nonetheless, until I dealt with this, I was not a sane person when accused. This is what we call a "trigger." Triggers are places where we have either repeatedly suffered a wound, or a wound has never been allowed to heal because it is situated in a place where people are going to keep bumping into it.

When we are uninjured, we can bump into people all day and we will hardly notice it. This is not the case when we are in pain. I remember the day I decided to get three piercings along the cartilage of my ear. Fueled by the teenage desire to impress my friends at school, I was determined. I had three earrings, a piece of ice, an alcohol swab, a safety pin, and a sense of reckless abandon. The first piercing was painful but endurable. Moments later, the second piercing nearly sent me through the roof. With a new respect for self-preservation, I did not attempt the third.

The piercings were extremely painful for at least a week. At first I remember thinking how bizarre it was that for years I had walked through the halls at school and people rarely, if ever, touched my ears. Yet now that I was in pain, it seemed that my ear was bumped at least a few times a day! By the fourth or fifth day of this, I realized how much kids bump into each other in high school hallways. I was only noticing it then because I was hurting. I had never noticed it before but now it infuriated me because I was already in pain.

We all have those things. Places that keep getting hurt. Places that when bumped into, get a bigger reaction than the bump warranted. These "triggers" are a sign of wounding. Triggers tell us where we are injured.

Dealing with smaller wounds quickly is an important part of preventing triggers. Many bigger issues start with a cut or a burn that did not get a chance to heal before being rubbed the wrong way or getting bumped into again. When you see someone--including yourself--being triggered it is time to become aware of the deeper issues at work.

Aware of Identity

Now allow me to introduce another important part of the overall metaphor--blood. Blood is our life-source. The DNA in our blood tells our body who we are. In forensic terms, blood is a certain way to identify us. The life-blood of our consciousness is our self-identity. Self-Identity is who you believe you are. To bring this together with First Aid MWE tools, let's take a deeper look into this.

When you think the phrase, "The me that is me," your pre-frontal cortex, the area of your brain right behind your forehead, should light up. I think of this area as the conscious equivalent of a physical heart. When we speak "from the heart", activity in our pre-frontal cortex will increase. Your pre-frontal cortex is the center of all decision making, and it is connected to virtually anything that helps you to be you. Emotion, memory, relationships, goals, desires, beliefs, and habits all connect back to this part of the brain. Much like the flow of blood through arteries and veins, these neurological connections keep everything we are alive, by flowing electrical impulses to and from other areas of the brain with information about our identity.

Interestingly, activity in the pre-frontal cortex has a direct effect on our heart. It not only affects our heart rate, but also the electromagnetic field that our heart produces. There's much to this dynamic connection, but for our purposes, we will focus on the fact that this neurologic system mimics the cardiovascular system in a very real way. We can learn much about our sense of identity and the systems which support it by drawing analogies from cardiovascular science. Bleeding, bruising, heart attacks, bone damage and respiratory failure all carry deeply metaphoric connections to identity.

The body's natural response to physical trauma is to rush blood to the area. In the same way, traumatic events, big or small, will activate the flow of thoughts from the pre-frontal cortex and apply them to the situation. This is where you will feel questions pulling on you (your pre-

33

frontal cortex) for a response: "Why did this happen?" and "How can I prevent this from happening again?" These are the primary aggravators, but the deeper question driving them is "Who am I?"

This is because how I respond to the pain is a reflection of who I am. The tangible connection between identity and crisis will inevitably tell me more about me. That is why we often see negative self images formed during traumatic events. Perhaps this is why we call those negative marks on our personalities "emotional scars."

When I don't have a satisfactory response to the questions that my mind is demanding answers to, the questions will simply remain present. This causes that emotional pain and swelling we feel when the area of pain is disturbed. Our instinct to avoid pain will lead us to avoid talking about it, avoid people who bump into it, and ultimately it will lead us to a closed off existence where the real me is unavailable.

This is an unnecessary and ultimately destructive lifestyle where the people who care about you can only know you and love you in pieces. You may think that your pain has made you "tough" but the truth is; unless you're free to be vulnerable, your pain has made a coward of you.

Stop ignoring. Stop avoiding. Pain is is not pointless. Pain will tell you where you are injured. Once you know how to treat the injury, you will relish the opportunity that painful situations provide. This is the first step, be aware.

B

BRUISING BURNS AND BLEEDING

<u>B</u>ruising <u>B</u>urns and <u>B</u>leeding

There are phrases, behaviors, and feelings that people consistently express, but few of us know what to do with them. Let's say that you are listening to a friend and by using the above clues, you have become "aware" that there is an issue. Stay calm. Stay warm. Stay engaged. This is going to be a good conversation.

The next three concepts will help you to understand what the flesh wound issue is and therefore determine your next step of action. There are easy to understand signs that will indicate the type of MWE flesh wound you are dealing with, the same way you recognize certain signs to indicate bruising, burns, and bleeding.

You are now going to come in contact with open wounds and you want to be "HELP-full." Now would be the time to prepare yourself with a "Heart Wash".

Next, ask questions that will help the real issue become clear. By asking about what they are experiencing, we find out what is going on internally rather than just discussing external judgments and opinions. Some good examples are:

"What was/is that like for you?"

"How are you feeling about that?"

"Are you learning anything about yourself because of that?"

These are useful, open ended questions that will tell you more about how your friend is experiencing a situation. As they respond, listen carefully with the intent to recognize the issues we are about to discuss. I will give you hints at how to recognize the issue in another or even in yourself.

About Trauma

In life you will run into hard situations or hard times will hit. When something happens to us that hurts, it is because our minds are having difficulty understanding it. If we understood it, we could process the shock and release it. When physical shock enters the body and cannot be released, we call it *trauma*. When emotional shock enters the mind and cannot be released, we call that *traumatic*. In short, trauma is unreleased shock.

Trauma comes in an entire spectrum of intensity and subsequent damage. Lighter trauma may cause a bruised ego; whereas intense or frequent trauma can cause deep brokenness. Physical trauma is gauged by how deeply it has affected our body. In the same way, emotional trauma can be gauged by how deeply it has affected our identity.

There are two basic kinds of trauma. Trauma A is trauma caused by the presence of a **negative** thing, such as an intense attack or onslaught of verbal and/or physical abuse. Trauma B is the absence of **positive** things such as never hearing "*I love you*" or the absence of praise and validation. Be aware of both as you listen for the symptoms of wounding in an MWE conversation.

It is important to be able to identify the level of trauma with which you are dealing. Deeply internal injuries will often require professional attention to fully resolve. First Aid MWE procedures will give you the tools to soothe light to average trauma as well as the ability to stabilize deeper brokenness. Trauma must be processed in order for us to move forward in life. Ignoring it can keep a person trapped in anxiety and even prevent the affected part of their personify from maturing. Trauma has the potential to reshape our personalities. It's effect can either be deeply negative or, with the right response, characteristically positive. Your first response to trauma can make all the difference in how the traumatic event will impact you or someone else. The first step is to identify trauma by recognizing unprocessed pain when you see it in others or even in yourself.

Be Able to Identify Bruising

The term "bruised ego" is thrown around quite a bit, and it is usually said in a dismissive way. This is not unlike the way we refer to light physical bruising: "It's just some bumps and bruises." Normally bruises are not a big deal. They are sore to the touch for a while and then they go away. Many ego bruisings are no different.

But realize that bruising, while mostly caused by pinches and bumps, can also be the result of being hit by a car or beaten with a bat. Bruises can be serious and even life threatening. So as you listen, remember that trauma, which bruises the emotional personality, can occur on a wide spectrum. Some bruises are very serious, like a bruise that covers an entire region of your personality or a bruise caused by a trauma that nearly fractures your bone (that inner resolve that protects your desire to live and to be you).

This kind of bruising is usually caused by an impact with a large moving object. The impact of an unexpected change of direction in an important part of your life: being fired, the death of a loved one, betrayal, divorce, rape, abuse, and miscarriage. These are examples of heavy things that can hit us very hard and bruise us to a point of disability.

A physical bruise is usually judged in severity by how much blood appears below the surface of the skin or how close to the bone the trauma reached. In the same way, a bruise to our emotional personality can be judged in severity by how much of our identity was stirred up and brought to our attention. Like the painful throb of a deep bruise, some part of our personality will hurt and we become painfully aware of it.

This pain is something we might describe as fear. It makes it hard to move. If I am bruised in the outgoing part of my personality, it makes meeting new people or being honest about myself painful and "nerve racking." If my sense of pride in myself (my spine) is bruised I might stiffen up and avoid "being soft" or a different kind of pain might keep me from "standing tall" so I take a low posture. Often we can even see these emotional issues manifest themselves in the body as a physical issue or posture.

A bruise to the body can be judged in severity by two things: 1. How much blood has surfaced to the skin? 2. How disabling is the pain of the bruise? Likewise, a bruise to the emotional personality can be judged in severity by looking at two things: 1. To what degree has this event shaken our sense of identity or caused us to question who we are? 2. How heavily has the trauma of the event affected our will to continue engaging with life?"

This concept should help you to identify when you are dealing with emotional bumps and bruises as well as enable you to differentiate between light and severe trauma.

Be Able to Identify Burns

Burns are usually unintentional or careless offenses. Someone says something hurtful to you, it burns. A minor burn stings, but rarely feels deeply wounding. Most of the time, once burned, we leave the situation to "cool off." This is an important first step that is oddly overlooked. If you are getting burned, get out.

The same way that friction causes substances to break down in a fire, when you spend too much time in a heated environment, you become "burnt out." Extreme relational friction will eventually cause the breakdown of our minds. We refer to serious burns like these as "total burnout." A total burnout often signals the overdue end of a relationship, a job, or an era in our lives.

Fully recovering from total burnout can take years. When we suffer severe burns, treatment becomes both more intense and drawn out. Remember this because we often want inner healing to be "one and done." In reality, first aid treatments are often a process repeated again and again until wounds finally disappear. Don't be discouraged when the same issue comes up again and again. It just means that it's time for another treatment. This is true for most serious wounds, and especially common when dealing with burns.

Be Able to Identify Bleeding

- **Cuts**
   A cut is often an intentional act or remark made by another person. A "cutting remark" implies that someone has knowledge of your vulnerabilities and has intentionally "cut you down." If a cut was made without you present, we refer to it as a "backstabbing." Not all cuts are intentional. Someone who truly cares about you can unintentionally cut you. Additionally, someone without any knowledge of your insecurities may be "sharp" with you, unintentionally cutting a place where you have not developed "thick skin." Cuts happen frequently. It's the reason we have so much language for it. They are usually small occurrences but they can certainly accumulate in situations where you work, live, or associate with cutters.

   Cuts will heal properly if they are identified, washed (forgiven), treated with ointment (deeper issue resolved), and bandaged (covered by a response plan). While small cuts can and will heal without help, any cut, regardless of size, can become infected-- if you do not forgive the cutter.

Small cuts that cause a big pain response are a sign of a compounding issue. There's more going on than just the cut. The disproportionate pain indicates a previous wound which has become a "trigger."

- **Abrasions**

Abrasions are mostly considered annoyances. We don't like personalities we consider abrasive. There are people who are going to "rub you the wrong way."

Like the difference between a cut and a scrape, a cut is usually one sharp slice, while an abrasion is a bunch of small little cuts. They are barely enough to notice individually, but all together they hurt like a burn. When someone clashes with us, we often say they "grate" on our nerves. When you get into an argument or debate, the rest of your day you might find yourself thinking about it, getting angry, having an imaginary round two. All those little fine cuts, those things that rub you the wrong way, those personality traits that grate on you, they add up to an abrasion. At times the offenses are so small we have difficulty defining them. In these cases we say things like, "I can't put my finger on what it is, but that guy really grates on me."

Abrasions are likely candidates for infection because they often come with the germs of judgement, anger, and unresolved feelings. The fact that they are difficult to define makes them difficult to clean. It's hard to let go of something that you can't put you finger on. This is why we recommend a good thorough cleaning with forgiveness whenever you see or feel abrasion.

C

C (See) The Memory

C The Memory

Now you have clues as to the issue being presented. So you can move on to looking at the wound itself and understanding how it got there. In this section I will give you some promptings that will help pinpoint important moments and memories as well as some tools to help you see those memories with ease.

Remember that word "hamartia?" I think of the moments we are looking for as moments of hamartia. They are formative experiences that have skewed the rails of our minds from being built on a healthy train of thought. These little changes in the angle we take on life may seem small. However, twenty years of building slightly off course can take us far from the happiness at which we had initially aimed ourselves.

Seeing a memory starts with a simple, "Try this." Encourage your friend or loved one to do whatever they need to do to focus. If this is not possible in that moment, you may want to tell them how to take the next steps in their own space, at a better time.

Best Practices for Memory Recall

Based on the visible symptoms, you may have a pretty good idea what kind of wound you are dealing with, but you cannot a treat a friend's wound without two things: 1. permission and 2. seeing the wound. You can't actually see the wound without seeing the memory where it occurred. You can't see the memory without permission. So your next step is important.

If you are speaking with a friend or loved one, let them know that you want to help if they're willing to let you try. Then you can ask:

"When was the first time that you felt that way?"

or

"When was the first time that happened to you?"

Encourage the person to share the very first memory that pops up when you ask your question, even if it seems unrelated. It is most likely spot on. The trick to all of MWE is that it's not you doing it. You are just asking good questions that stimulate the natural will of every person to thrive.

The key memory should come quickly and spontaneously to the surface. If it is from early childhood, it is likely an original wound. These are the most important because, recalling our railroad analogy, they determine the initial direction of our thought lives.

As a note: If it takes more than twenty seconds or so to think of something, then the memory that comes up may be contrived. This is still a real memory deserving of respect and attention. However if it is contrived rather than spontaneous, it may not be the actual or original wound. If this memory does have a wound in it, you can deal with it, knowing that there may still be more to look at later. This happens most when we are not quite ready to "open up old wounds." Once we experience how great it feels to get wounds cleaned out and bandaged, we will get a little more free to open up.

Tips For Memory Recall

It's often best to close your eyes if you are comfortable doing so and then recall the memory out loud from beginning to end. As you do this immerse yourself in the memory. Be there as vividly as your mind will allow you to be.

This will fire energy into the dendrites containing the memory and also light up the neural pathways closely connected to it. The more vividly we can recall the memory and the feelings associated with it, the more effective the detox step (which comes next) will be. Sometimes by simply listening to ourselves tell the story, we will begin to hear the issues within.

Doing this with a friend can increase the probability of finding the issues, as it's often easier to see more clearly from the outside looking in. At the same time, when you are helping a friend, don't assume that all the issues you think you see from the outside are actual issues or that they are all ready to be removed. If you think you see something, simply ask. Remember that First Aid MWE is mostly questions and has very little content. We do this to give those we are assisting full authority over what is happening. This empowers them to decide what they will and will not get into. It is their journey of discovery, and they must choose their own pace of healing.

The Blank Page (Creating a Clean Workspace)

Maybe you are ready to move forward but your thoughts are too cluttered. Perhaps the idea that a response will appear by simply asking a question is too unfamiliar. You may wonder: Where will it appear? How will I know the answer when it's there? If that is the case, it can be extremely helpful to practice using the screen of your mind by way of this next exercise.

This is a basic exercise intended to familiarize the mind with accessing memory, feeling, and free thought. First aid cannot be properly done in a cluttered or dirty environment. The Blank Page Tool helps to clear and focus the screen of the mind. This makes First Aid MWE procedures easier and more effective. You can come back to this simple tool any time you are having trouble focusing.

HERE ARE THE STEPS:

Start by spending 5-20 minutes in complete silence or listening to nature sounds. If you find it difficult to quiet your mind, that is understandable; don't struggle. Struggle will defeat the purpose of this time. Let the thoughts pass through your mind. Watch them come and go as one observing the activity in your mind rather than being caught up in the activity itself. As you observe the thoughts, you will realize that you are not your thoughts; you are something else. Feel yourself in that place where there is a distance between you and the thoughts that happen to be in your mind. The space where you see the thoughts coming and going is the screen. When the timing feels right, you may begin.

It is important not to interfere with the images or senses you are about to experience in your mind. Answer these next questions one at a time without overthinking. Read one question, pause, and say **out loud** the very first answer that comes to your mind. (The "out loud" part is important. It doesn't have to be LOUD, just loud enough for you to hear yourself say it.)

First, I want you to focus your attention on the screen of your mind. The screen of your mind is that place where thoughts form. This is where you see your memories, where you have dreams and day dreams, and where you imagine.

To help actualize this place, I want you to imagine a blank page. Do you see the page? Can you get a sense that it is there?

If you see the page...(What does it look like?)

Do you sense it there?...(Describe what you sense.)

Is it in a binder or looseleaf?...

Run your finger across the surface of the page. Is it textured or smooth?...
(What does it feel like?)

Can you smell the paper?... (What does that smell remind you of?)

Can you hear the sound it makes when you move it?...(Describe the
sound.)

This place, not the paper, but the space where you see, feel, hear,
or sense the paper-- that is the screen of your mind. Right now the blank
page may feel like a faint impression of a thing. The screen is not the
thing you see in your mind, it is the space that the thing occupies.

From this point, you can empty that space and proceed with
whatever it is you want to work on. You will find this concept to be a useful
launch pad from which to begin any kind of mental exercise. If you ask a
question and nothing comes into the screen, you may use the blank page
to draw on. If you have difficulty seeing anything coming into the screen
you can begin by "drawing" the answers on your blank page.

Run through these questions as many times as you need, in order
to get used to the spontaneous answers that will come into your screen. If
you're not sure how to see something spontaneously, simply say any
answer as quick as possible. I've heard it said that, "In your brain, your
'imaginator' is parked right next to your 'revelator.'" I can say from
experience that this seems to be true. So long as you keep a discerning
eye on what is coming to mind, do not worry if it feels like you're using
your imagination. This is a place where revelation, dreaming, creativity,
and envisioning your future plans will occur. We find solutions to our
problems by allowing ourselves to interact with that empty page of

creativity. Everything that comes to the screen, good, bad, or indiscernible is evidence of what is in your mind. Learn to work with it as it comes.

Keep in mind that the responses we are hoping for should feel fresh, life giving, revelatory, and even surprising. If you pose a question but what comes to your page is negative, oppressive, or judgmental, you are probably overthinking the answer and allowing your pain to respond with cynicism. If this is the case, walk yourself through the forgiveness exercise found in this manual. Repeat the forgiveness exercise over and over thinking of as many people as you can muster up. When you have done this sufficiently you will notice a significant change in the content that comes to the screen of your mind.

Remember when you are asking a question that the answer should feel as though it appeared out of nowhere. We don't want to know what your conscious mind has to say. We want the answers to come from a deeper place. By simply posing a question and waiting, answers will well up from the place in your mind where your thoughts flow seamlessly with the unconscious will to live, thrive, and to know love. Holding on to judgments and withholding forgiveness places barriers between you and your ability to live, thrive, and know love because your will to live, thrive, and to know love is indelibly anchored to your will for others to live, thrive, and to know love. Thus forgiveness is the key to unbinding and unblinding yourself.

Now that the screen is clear, you can ask again.

"When was the first time I felt _____ Describe your pain _____ ?"

(Describe the memory that comes to mind)

D

DETOXIFY

Detoxify

Once you are in a memory, many issues can be resolved or at least begin to heal by answering these five basic detoxifying questions:

1. Who do I need to forgive? 2. What lies did I begin to believe? 3. What judgments did I accept? 4. What inner vows did I make? 5. What was the contract I agreed to?

I will explain each one and how to address them.

Understanding How Infection Starts

Every kind of wound presents some opportunity for infection by toxic thoughts. The swelling of emotion brings with it questions about why we are having this negative experience. Without clear answers, our minds will grab on to any possible explanation and then that explanation will integrate itself into our decision making matrix.

That question "why?" is not unlike the moisture of an open wound. Asking "why did this happen?" keeps our identity fluid and adaptable. This can ultimately bring healing, but it can also unintentionally grab on to a foreign invader hiding in the grit and grime of the world.

Infection spreads when a false explanation invades our personality. For example, let's say that Sally is molested by an older boy at a young age. Sally's mind is reeling for answers: "Why did he do that? Why did my body respond that way? Why me and not my sister?" An adult could likely investigate the situation and understand the answers, but Sally could not.

Let's say we know the answers: He did it because he was emulating something that happened to him. The physical response Sally felt was due to the stimulation of autonomous nerves, and the reason he chose her was because he believed she was less likely to resist or tell on him.

Sally's mind was looking for those answers, but she came up with a completely different set. "Why did he do that?" she asked. Then she remembered her Mom telling her to be more careful about how she played when she was wearing a dress. She recalled that she had not been careful. "That must be why! This was my fault." she concluded. "I hope my mom doesn't find out. I might get in trouble." "What was that strange way that my body responded?" she asks herself. The answer seems obvious to her, "I must have liked it a little. Maybe I'm bad," she pondered. "Why did he choose me and not my sister?" The final question now falling down like a domino in a line, and the answer fitting right into the space created by the expanding lies. "Maybe, he could see that I was a bad girl." or "Maybe he thinks I'm prettier than her and that's how boys show you that you are special." We can now see the track being laid out before Sally. So long as this infection remains unchecked, the road ahead is bound to be destructive for both her and for the people who love her.

This demonstrates an interesting function of our brain. We will talk more about how these judgments are formed further on. Suffice it to say, that this survival mechanism seems to help us adapt to physical circumstances, but it causes all kinds of issues when applied to abstract thinking. Once we suspect something to be true, our brain looks for proof

48

to validate that belief. Sally's "answers" become like lenses through which she views herself and the world around her. The more she sees the world through these lenses of false assumption, the more validated she will feel in her belief. As her mind settles on her answers to the trauma, a new behavior will surface.

Memories build the primary neural pathways for decision making. Information cannot overcome this system, because information is not stored in the same way as memories. Information is not integrated into the primary pathways our brain creates for decision making. We can reference knowledge when making a decision, but ultimately our core process for decisions comes down to our collection of experiences and the emotional tags we associate with them. This makes all the sense in the world. "Eating fruit satisfies me. I feel good. I like fruit. I will eat fruit again." The problem is when we use this same system to make sense of things that only exist in our own abstract ideas of the world. "I am hungry. I don't have food. You have food. I will take your food. Stealing makes me feel powerful. I like stealing. I am a thief."

Unchecked, an infection's ultimate destination is our self-image. This can have a profound effect on our decision making. As we observe a repeated behavior that we now have difficulty resisting, the infection reaches bone -- our will to be the person that we believe we are. If our will is weakened, we will soon accept the infection as an identity.

Not to fear, in this section I will show you simple habits and exercises that can remove and reverse the effects of infection from the oldest of wounds. This is where the timelessness of memory becomes advantageous.

Four Kinds of Infection

Infectious agreements come in a diverse spectrum; yet they all work from a common principal. They are toxic underlying beliefs that we unwittingly adopt in order to understand our experiences. To make

49

identifying these agreements easier, I have categorized them into four overlapping concepts: lies, vows, judgments, and contracts. Once we have identified the type of infection, we will know how to clean it.

• **Lies**

A lie is something that we are told or what we inferred from a situation that ultimately is not true. Lies embed themselves into memories and can affect behavior, even if the truth becomes obvious with age and maturity. The more destructive lies tend to answer the question, "Why?": "Why don't the other kids want to hang out with me?" "Why was I the one this happened to?" "Why did Mom say that to me?" The most destructive lies will still feel true to us in our adulthood.

• **Vows**

A vow is something you declare, either out loud or internally, to yourself. Destructive vows are usually made in the wake of betrayal, judgment, or bitterness: "I will never...", "From now on I will always...", "He/She will never...", "He/She will always...", "I wish I could kill him/her/ myself." Many times these vows seem meaningless; they are not.

Vows take a simplistic mechanism meant to help us adapt to constants and applies it to complex emotional issues. This simple mechanism inspired by negative emotion is helpful in preventing mistakes such as eating poisonous berries. The response is: "I will never eat those again!" When applied to pain from a relationship: "I will never trust you again." This could set the course for constant struggle against oneself. Vows have strong influence because they tap into our instinctive survival tools. Add to that the fact that vows are most often attached to a memory tagged with negative emotion. No amount of knowledge can make you "unlearn" that vow. You need to tap into the memory and break agreement with the vow. (I will cover this under "Breaking Agreements".)

• Judgments

A judgment is a conclusive determination about a thing. It works on a similar principle to a vow. Judgements help us to adapt to our environment, stay alive, and accomplish goals. For example: I see a coconut. I throw a rock at it. I miss. Glutamate is released into my system, and now I feel disappointed. I adjust my aim and thrust. I miss again. I get a larger dose of glutamate. I look at the rock. I think, "This rock may be too small." I try with a larger rock. I succeed. Dopamine flushes my system. I feel happiness. I think, "Little rock bad. Big rock good." The judgment attaches to the memory. I now grab only big rocks for this job. The result: I eat more coconuts and survive.

Now, we take the same principal and apply it to our self-identity. I try algebra; I get confused. Problem after problem, I keep missing the answer. I feel like I'm failing. With every wrong answer, more glutamate is released into my system. I feel disappointment and a need to ask, "Why?" Here comes the judgment: "I am not good at math." I am now treating my potential as if it is a rock used to gather coconuts. The major difference is I don't have other brains to throw at the problem. In truth, if I am willing to keep working at it, I can be great at math. The judgment that I cannot is now an infection that will trigger the release of negative emotions every time I attempt algebra. Boo.

Judgments can come at us both internally or externally: "You'll never amount to anything." "You're ugly." "You aren't funny." "Art...math...science... love... just isn't your thing." These judgments are most powerful when you already have high levels of negative hormones in your system. Such as in the midst of a crisis, a disappointment, or during any formative stage of maturity.

Judgments also work against us when we apply them to others. In the same way that we assess a big or little rock to be useful, we also tend to assess people according to our needs. Again, this process does not seem to be adaptive beyond its usefulness in survival. There is a very unique principal that comes into play when we judge others. We've all heard the saying, "Judge not, lest you be judged." This principal actually works on a very powerful level in our own psychology. This is what I call a "mimetic transference." That's just a fancy way of saying that we judge others more harshly in areas where we have a similar weaknesses in ourselves. It's our lack of self acceptance that makes it impossible for us to accept certain others. We tend to dislike the most, those who reflect our own weaknesses. When we hold onto judgments, we actually prevent ourselves from overcoming the same potential issue in ourselves. This often means that we will blindly propagate the same issues and behaviors in our own lives. How many of us have judged our parents issues and then blindly walked right into repeating their faults?

Our knee jerk reaction to this revelation might be to cut ourselves off from making any negative judgments, but ultimately that would only be a complex form of denial. Making judgments is a necessary survival instinct. The solution here is to stay aware of all the judgments we make of others. When you catch yourself judging, release the other person from that fault and then release yourself from the same thing, as if the thing you judged them for was a fault of your own. It likely is. Forgiving others for their faults and choosing to see them according to their potential will help you overcome your own faults and live up to more of your own potential.

Remember, the next time someone gets under your skin, it might be you, the one who is actually under you skin, that is truly offending. Having grace and patience for others enables us to have it for ourselves and thus we move on to developing a healthier identity. With this knowledge we can catch ourselves judging and use those moments to gain insight into our own potential faults.

- **Contracts**

A contract is a bond formed out of powerlessness. At its root, it is an agreement such as a lie, vow, or judgment. Think of it as a relationship contract. A healthy core for a relationship would be, "I choose you." The core of a contractual relationship is, "I need _____ from you," and/or "you need _____ from me." This may sound fair, but it is a set up for countless problems. Ultimately, we are putting our sense of value/happiness/contentment into someone else's hands. This is dangerous for them because most likely, they did not agree to our expectations. It's unhealthy for us because someone else is not capable of meeting our core needs. This is power we should not give to another person.

Don't worry, this doesn't mean that you need to end the relationships that have functioned this way. It does mean that you are about to change for the better. You are about to become a more powerful person. You do not need any of your relationships to be based on this type of contract.

A tell-tale sign of a contract is when a person has an undue influence on your emotions. They can pull you up; that's when the contract feels like a great idea. Or they can pull you down-- into their mess. That's when you start to wonder why they have so much power over your emotions.

Contracts are formed when your emotional needs are met by another person. This is not bad in and of itself. We are interdependent creatures who will die without bonds formed between us. The problem is when those bonds are formed on the basis of a lie, inner vow, or judgment. It's in these moments when we fail to manage ourselves because we contract the job to someone else.

Let's say we find ourselves attracted to something in a person. *Something we believe we cannot produce ourselves.* (This is a lie.) In truth, only we can manage our own emotions. Only we can produce the contentment that we crave. When we try to give that job to someone else, we chose to contract out our sense of security. Therefore our peace becomes dependent upon another person. I call this activity "climbing." We do this when we believe that it is easier than maintaining the emotion for ourselves. This is dangerous for both people involved. The moment we feel disconnected from the contracted person, our confidence plummets and our peace is disrupted. This leads to offense: we feel they didn't keep their end of the deal (which they probably never agreed to do). The issue with climbing is that healthy people find their own footing and do not use others to get to the top.

Let's say someone expresses appreciation for you. *The value they put on you makes you feel confident and happy.* You may choose to believe the lie that you need them to value you in order to be happy. (In truth, only you can make yourself feel valuable and thus confident and content.) If we give into this lie, then we will contract out our confidence and subsequently how happy we are with ourselves. (i.e. I will be or do things that you appreciate so that you respond and make me feel valued.) This is dangerous for both of you. When you feel unappreciated by the other, your confidence plummets and is usually replaced by offense. I call this activity "pyramid building." **The issue with pyramid building is that healthy people build themselves up by focusing on their intrinsic value, not the wavering perceptions of others.**

Both climbing and pyramid building are styles of codependence. Think of codependence as using, and therefore depending on, someone else to make ourselves feel powerful. The difference between these two styles is that a pyramid builder will try to collect people they see as weak, and then stand on them. While a climber will try to find people they see as powerful and climb on their backs.

When a pyramid builder meets a climber, they look like two people trying to use each other as a life raft. The builder tries to stand on top of the admiration of the climber. While the climber tries to climb up on the success of the builder. As long as they are both contractually obligated by their perceived needs, they will perpetually disappoint and frustrate each other. This is not the recipe for a thriving relationship.

These unspoken contracts can become deeply complicated. The emotional needs we assign to others often have their root in unmet parental bonds. These unmet needs are tangled in a mess of memory and emotion. When you see a contract in your life, remember this helpful information. Contracts are often a good indication that something deeper needs your attention. The beauty of dealing with the contract first is that this frees us to untangle the deeper problem without the painful contract hooked into our emotional personality. Thankfully, contracts are not unlike lies, vows, and judgments. They are simply another type of unhealthy agreement. We can deal with all of them in almost the same way.

Now we know what issues to look for in a memory: 1. Who do I need to forgive? 2. What lies did I begin to believe? 3. What judgments did I accept or make? 4. What inner vows did I make? and/or 5. What emotional need did i assign to that person? With these questions now securely in our First Aid Kit, let's discuss the actual steps to Detoxify.

Forgiveness (Cleaning Wounds)

The first step to detoxification is to wash the wound. Here is where we introduce an important part of the First Aid metaphor-- water. Forgiveness is the clean water of MWE care. Many believe that forgiveness is something they do for someone else. This could not be more wrong. To withhold forgiveness is to withhold treatment for yourself. To wait for the offender to apologize in order to forgive is like waiting to care for your wounds until the person who stabbed you provides the treatment. This may never happen. Forgiving others is actually for you.

Forgiveness stops damage in its tracks and keeps your wounds clean and free from the infection of bitterness. Withholding forgiveness is like saying, "I won't let go of these germs until their rightful owner removes them." This stubbornness would only hurt you.

In the same way that there's a proper way to clean a wound effectively, there are also specific steps in forgiveness. Doing forgiveness right helps us to truly let go of the lies, vows, judgments, and contracts that threaten to infect our otherwise healthy personalities.

STEPS TO FORGIVE:

Begin by focusing your attention on the screen of your mind. Are you there?... Ask this question out loud: "Who do I need to forgive?"

Most likely, you will quickly see a face, hear a name, think of a voice, or simply have a knowledge of who it is.

At this point you may want to back out-- don't. You need this, and you're ready, otherwise you wouldn't have seen it. If you're getting nothing, don't worry. Things pop up on the screen when you need and are ready for them.

Now you will speak as though you are speaking directly to the person you need to forgive. Feel free to be vulnerable and honest about your feelings and how they hurt you. Finish these sentences:

(Person), you hurt me when you...

That hurt me because...

I needed you to...

When I didn't get that from you, I...

Once these sentences are completed, take a moment to grieve what you have lost.Think of grief as an ice pack. Intentional grieving is important for both pain management as well as for reducing the swelling of your identity into a situation. Deeply grieve what is deeply painful and you will find it easier to let it go and move on.

Take a moment to do that now.

56

Now it's time to **wash it clean** with forgiveness.

(Person), I realize now that you cannot fix the damage that was done inside of me. I won't expect you to.

(Person), I forgive you. I release you from the judgements I made of you. As of today, you owe me nothing.

Take a moment to let that sink in...

Now that the wound is cleaned and cooled, we can remove debris.

Breaking Agreements (Identifying and Removing Debris)

You have recollected the wound and washed it with forgiveness, so now you can identify any lies, vows, judgments, or contracts that took hold in that moment. Think of them as debris: dirt, grit, or other foreign objects in the wound. These can quickly cause pain, infection, and in more severe cases-- deformity of the mind, will, or emotion. Left unaddressed, they can eventually cause a loss of limb (losing part of ourselves) forever. Often these lies, especially the ones with smooth edges that sound true, can sit beneath the surface of our personality, undetected until we put pressure on them. Uncovering and removing them safely is an important part of First Aid MWE.

Now, ask one of these questions:

- *"What is a **lie** that I began to believe at this time?"*

- *"What **vow** did I make at this time?"*

- *"What is a **judgment** that I made at this time?"*

- *"What power did I give away at this time?" (**contract**)*

(If more than one question fits the memory, you can proceed with just one and then return to this point and proceed with another.)

Listen quietly for a moment and go with the first thing that comes to mind. Remember that you are reporting aloud and not editing the thoughts/pictures that come to your screen. If it doesn't sound like something you currently believe, remember that you didn't ask about what you currently think you believe. You asked about what the you in the memory started to believe at that time.

Now, say the (lie, vow, judgment, or contract) out loud.

LIE: Repeat after me, "I break agreement with the lie that____(repeat the lie)____. That was not true."

VOW: Repeat after me, "I break agreement with the vow that____(repeat the vow)____. That vow did not help me."

JUDGMENT: Repeat after me, "I break agreement with the judgment that____(repeat the judgment)____. That was judgment was not true."

CONTRACT: Repeat after me, "I break agreement with the contract that____(repeat the contract)____. That contract was not necessary."

Repeat the "Breaking Agreement" steps until each lie, vow, judgment and contract is dealt with.

E

EXCHANGE

Exchange

Once you break an agreement based on one of your detoxifying questions, an exchange can take place. You will want to do at least one exchange for each agreement you have broken. By doing this, toxic thoughts can be replaced by helpful thoughts in one simple step, creating an anti-bacterial shield that stops the growth of new infections.

Once the exchange is complete, that formative memory in the brain will connect to the positive experience of healing the issue. The memory is already part of an established pathway that helps guide decision making. So while there may or may not be a strong emotional response to the exchange itself, time will reveal the overall impact of the experience.

Trading Up (Applying Anti-Bacterial Ointment)

Now that we have identified the debris, we need remove it and close the wound. When we remove something unclean, we replace it with something that will kill the germs of destructive emotions and beliefs. Think of this as removing debris and then filling the void with anti-bacterial ointment. It's simple and intuitive. You will know what needs to go. You will watch it go, and then what you need will come to replace it.

HERE ARE THE STEPS:

Start this stage by picturing the lie, vow, judgment, contract that you have broken agreement with. See it as a thing that you can hold in your hands. You may see a vivid metaphor that you can contemplate later or you may not see anything. If you can feel like you have the lie, vow, judgment, or contract in your hands, you're ready to move forward.

At this point, you may see something negative that you have no problem letting go. In contrast, you may see something that is important to you but you have made protecting it a source of fear and stress. Releasing these valuable things (relationships, jobs, children) does not mean that we don't care. Rather, we are embracing the journey of life and letting go of that which we cannot control; which is everything but ourselves. **What we are doing is releasing the false responsibilities connected to these things, not necessarily the things themselves. Often in** this step, people will see a person representing God who they can trust to take care of the thing they let go of. If you see this too, go with it even if you don't necessarily believe in God. Trust yourself and trust that you are seeing what you need to see.

Now that you see it in your hands, hold it out and say, "I do not want to carry this anymore, will you come and take this?"

You may or may not see someone there, but the thing in your hand will disappear in some way.

Is it gone? (If it remains, you will know that you are not ready to let go of it yet. That's okay. Take a moment to consider what need it may be meeting in your life.)

If you see it leaving, watch as it goes. What's happening to it? How is it being dealt with? What you see will often be a symbolic insight.

Now, whether it is gone or not, ask, "What do you want to give me instead?"

You will (see, hear, feel, sense, know) something coming to replace the thing you let go.

What is it? Describe it. Consider how it would replace the thing you let go (or are considering letting go).

If you have not let go yet, try again. See what happens.

Now, let the new thing come and ask it to fill every space that the thing you let go of previously occupied. Take a moment to describe what it feels like to have new thing replace the old.

Once each lie, vow, judgment or contract has been exchanged, you can see any outlying issues you may need to deal with. These are things that may not be defined by "lie, vow, judgment, or contract", but they are interrelated issues and emotions such as fear, trauma, need to control, etc. You can let go of these attached issues by asking, "What else do I need to let go of?" Then picture your hands and the thing you need to release will appear in them or you may simply realize what else you need to release. If nothing comes to mind, then move on to the final stage, "Follow Through Bandaging."

If you are able to see the one who takes it, feel free to follow your curiosity about that person and see how much you can learn.

Finally, take a moment to be thankful for the experience you just had. Thankfulness is a very important part of this tool, so take your time with it. Picture yourself expressing the thankfulness you feel. When that feels complete, you are done.

Here's a fun optional additional step:

Go back into the memory where you began. Once there, you will say, "I invite truth to come into this memory and show me something new."

Wait for truth to show up as a person. Spend as much time with truth as you like and ask as many questions as you want. Our brains are hard wired for relationship, so interacting with truth as a person rather than a concept allows you to use a more powerful thought processing system than the area of your brain dedicated to processing abstract thoughts. Incredibly, when doing this, most people will describe the interaction as a deeply spiritual experience.

If you have trouble seeing anything here, try using "The Wall Tool." (coming up)

Before leaving the memory, ask truth if you can come back and meet him here. If truth thinks this is a good idea, open up your scope of view and look around the place you see in the memory. It will often transform and become a secure place for you to meet with truth and get clarity, anytime that you want on any matter.

Detoxing and Exchanging A Trigger

If you think about how many early memories have faded or disappeared, you will realize that the ones you remember are probably important and meaningful to you. When a memory keeps popping up, it's doing that for a reason. Use the detox and exchange tools we just learned to explore the memory. In doing so you will likely discover why the memory stayed with you and how it is relevant to your current situations in life.

In the same way, we carry around "triggers" for a reason. We carry unresolved pain that will continue to affect us until we address it. When you feel "triggered" (something bumps into a painful place in you), make a mental note to remember the circumstances. Describe to yourself, in words, the way you are feeling. Once you are ready, you can use the following questions to launch directly into the Detox step in order to remove the source of original pain free yourself of the trigger.

HERE ARE THE STEPS:

Ask, preferably out loud, *"When was the first time I felt this way?"* or *"When was the first time I learned to _____(describe your bad response to the situation) when _____(describe the circumstances that caused the bad reaction.)"*

Some good examples are:

"When was the first time I learned <u>to use anger to defend myself</u> when <u>someone suspects me</u>?"

"When was the first time I learned to <u>make important relationships insecure</u> when <u>I feel insecure</u>?")

Once you ask the question, wait quietly. The memory you need to explore will come to your screen. Once you have a memory to work with, you can go straight to the Detox step, **starting with forgiveness.**

F

FOLLOWTHROUGH

Followthrough

I like to conclude any memory interactions with a friend by asking them to tell me what they plan on doing the next time they face the same issue. If it's me working through something alone, I say my plan out loud. That should fire up the mental network involved in the issue and reinforce the new information into the thought process.

There are so many variables in a person's overall mental health, and you cannot be responsible for them. Sometimes a simple interaction will change a person's life. Other times, it will be a small contribution to a larger spectrum of issues for that person to overcome. Know that you have done what you can with the tools that you have. Even if it is a small contribution, you have done so much more than offer up an empty platitude. You've been real; you've been true to your heart; that's what life is all about: you chose to do good to another person.

Followthrough is the Bandage

Now that you have throughly explored the issues in the memory, you can "wrap it up" by creating a plan for how to deal with the prevailing issues that came forward during detoxifying and exchanging.

Let's say that we discovered a memory of the first time I developed a fear of judgement. I looked at the memory and realized that I began to believe the lie that I should not "be myself" around others. I tried to see the lie in my hands and it looked like a small sword. Upon thinking about what that could mean, I thought about how I might be using some sharp personality traits to discourage people from judging me. I gave up the sword and in return, I saw honesty drip on my forehead like a huge drop of light. It lit up my face and made me look quite handsome. So now I want to ask a followthrough question.

"What should I do the next time I am afraid that I am being judged?"

I wait quietly for the answer to spontaneously arise.

Maybe I help it along by imagining myself with a glowing face looking at a person who I believe is judging me. Then, I see myself speaking honestly, candidly, and fearlessly. It feels powerful to be saying exactly what I am thinking and feeling. Though I am being honest, I do not feel vulnerable because I know that I have already accepted who I am. I can hear myself saying it: "I accept who I am. It's okay to be me. If other people don't like me, that is their problem to deal with not mine." Suddenly it sounds crazy to me that I had tried to manage each and every person's opinion of me.

Now you try it. I want you to ask, "What should I do the next time _____ (describe the appropriate situation for your exchange)?"

Wait quietly for the answer to spontaneously arise. The response you hear will be the bandage that will protect the wound from re-injury, keeping it safe and clean until this new experience is securely fixed in your decision making memory matrix.

If during the course of this journey you stirred up more than one memory, you can undergird and strengthen the positive change you just made by repeating the process for each one.

If during the course of this journey you saw, sensed, or heard answers that seemed like they had deeper meanings, use the screen of your mind to go back there and ask more questions about it.

The Wall Tool

You may find that you are progressing through the steps of an exercise when suddenly it feels as though you've hit a wall. You intend to move forward, but something is holding you back. This is usually a sign that you are not ready for the next step. We put up walls for our own protection. This is much like the way we might assume a tense posture to protect a painful wound. In many cases it's a smart thing to do, but when you need to move forward and you hit a wall it means you need to pause and ask yourself, "why?" The wall tool is designed to discover just that. The wall tool can help you progress beyond defense mode and into healing the actual wound.

As an added bonus, you can also use the wall tool anytime you feel like something is blocking you from moving forward in life. This tool will help you identify the wall, see why it is there, learn if there's a healthier way to protect yourself, and remove the blockage.

HERE ARE THE STEPS:

Ask aloud, "Is there a wall that I have put up between me and _____(Describe what you are trying to get to. i.e. this memory, the voice of truth, life, God, forgiveness, love.)?"

You will either sense a wall or you will sense what seems like nothingness. The presence of nothing in a mind that is constantly thinking, is suspicious. Nothing is something. Always be suspicious of nothing.

What does the wall look/feel like? Describe it. (This may mean describing what it feels like to look out into nothingness.) You may feel an emotion rather than seeing wall. Pay attention to your body. How does the wall make your body feel? Describe that.

Now name the wall based on what you described. (Common names are, wall of fear, wall of judgment, wall of anger, wall of sarcasm, wall of cynicism, wall of denial, wall of emptiness.)

Now ask, "How have I used a wall of _____ to protect me?"

You might see a memory at this point. You might just know the answer to that question. You might get a slew of memories.

For clarity ask, "When was the first time I used a wall of _____ to protect me?"

Take this new memory and proceed with the rest of the steps (Detox, Exchange, and Followthrough) using that memory.

Once you are done you can command the wall to come down.

To command the wall down, just say, "Wall of _____ I don't need you to protect me anymore. When I clap you are going to fall down." **CLAP**

The clapping gives you a good moment to expect the wall to come down, and the startling sound helps snap the synapses that hold the wall together in your brain.

Once the wall is down, see if you can discover what's on the other side. If there's a beautiful place on the other side, go in and ask truth, life, God, etc. to come and talk with you there.

With the wall down, you can now pick up where you left off when you originally found the wall blocking you. (This is where it may be handy to take a few notes as you go through the steps. If you don't remember, that's okay too. Maybe the wall was the real issue that needed to be dealt with today.)

If you used the wall tool because you couldn't get to a memory, see if that memory is there on the other side of the wall. You can invite truth into the memory and/or move on to the detox step.

PART 2

INTERNAL ISSUES

RECOGNIZE AND RESPOND

Internal Issues

Internal issues are our second category of issues. These will each have a unique First Aid MWE response. A first responder is one who is equipped to stabilize an issue long enough to create a plan for long term care. The responses for these three issues are meant to be a stabilization technique rather than a long term solution. These issues do not follow the ABCDEF model. Rather each one is presented here in two phases "recognize" and "respond."

The ability to recognize what is going on inside of a person is a huge advantage in any relationship. Your best course of action when you suspect that you know what's going on is to respectfully ask about it. When a problem arises in you or someone you love, your first goal is not to fix it. It is to understand it. Take the time to ask clarifying questions before you assume to understand the issue. Do remember that even if you think you know what the issue is, you might not. First we must recognize what we are dealing with and then we can respond appropriately. Now let's look at how to recognize and respond to these specific internal issues.

MWE Heart Attack

Recognizing an MWE Heart Attack

Earlier we described the pre-frontal cortex as the heart of our personality. It's a crude analogy, but it works. In more specific terms, the system that handles emotions and social interactions is composed of many different parts such as the basal ganglia, the thalamus, the amygdala, the cingulate cortex, the right-sided prefrontal cortex, and the left sided prefrontal cortex. If the prefrontal cortex is the heart, then we can think of this larger network as the cardiovascular system of the brain. In the same way that your blood carries oxygen and DNA to keep your body alive. The thoughts flowing from this network connect your identity (i.e. your self-awareness) to the things you are experiencing and bring them to life for you. MRI scans during a complex relational interaction will show the greater part, if not all, of this network becoming active. The scans also reveal that we have significant pathways dedicated to connecting these identity forming areas with another network of the brain; our mimetic network.

So what do these mimetic areas of our brain do? Think of mimesis as shared desire. Mimesis is the process of learning what we want by observing what others want. It is a major part of everything formative in our sense of self. Without connection, relationship, and mimesis, ultimately we would have no identity. Theoretically without a foundation of relationships, we would have no sense of self at all. This is why relational pain will directly and immediately affect our personal identity.

Have you ever heard the expression, "She just lost it"? What did she lose? How about, "Get control of yourself?" If I am not in control, then who is? Another one would be, "He blew a fuse." Where is this fuse box? Evidently it needs fuses that can handle higher voltages! These colloquial terms are hints at what's going on inside of us when we exceed our emotional capacity.

We exceed our emotional capacity when our perceived problems exceed the strength of our internal social/emotional network. When that happens, activity shifts away from the prefrontal cortex and increases in the area known as the "reptilian brain." It's kind of like having a backup system in case of outages and emergencies. This is the part of our brain that is largely instinctual, animalistic, and simple. This shift is called a "fight or flight" response and it happens for two main reasons: to keep you alive in an actual emergency and for the reason previously stated, because of an emotional overload. In First Aid MWE, we call these emotional overloads "Heart Attacks." The heart of your personality overloads and all systems shift to your emergency backup brain.

For reptiles, the reptilian brain is all they have. Our reptilian brain is the primary brain we use during fight or flight mode. We can think of this mode as T-Rex mode. When we are in T-Rex mode, we have a big mouth with sharp teeth and we have powerful legs to run down threats. If we choose flight, we will use all of our power and speed to run away. In this state of mind, we lose touch with our prefrontal cortex. When "she lost it," that's what she lost-- her identity, and by proxy of identity, her sense of relationship to others. It's a heart attack. In this mode you have no heart to share with others. The you that is you is not in control anymore because your social and emotional "cardiovascular" system could not handle the load of your thoughts.

During an emotional heart attack, we lose **power** to the part of our brain that tells us who we are and connects us to the relationships and desires that we share with the people we know. That power is incrementally redirected to the reptilian brain. All of us have experienced this to some degree: your pulse rises, your body tenses, your thoughts fill almost exclusively with possible threats and your responses to those threats. This is great for surviving a wild animal attack, but not good for our jobs, friendships, finances, or marriages. This is your brain on fear.

74

Things can get worse and stay worse when we unintentionally integrate fear into our higher level decision making. Fear responses can network with memories by piggybacking on lies, judgments, and vows. This is how we can get stuck in varying levels of "T-Rex mode." This typically occurs when the shock of a painful event has no explanation and therefore no way to escape our mind. This makes it impossible for us to think clearly as our true selves, once we have been triggered. The emotional/social network becomes dependent on fear responses to make decisions. So now every time we try to make a decision, our brain begins to imagine everything that could go wrong and then how we would respond to that threat. No surprise that the responses provided by our lower brain are usually either aggressive or evasive, that's just what it does. This is not the thinking of a powerful person. Our heart is in distress and needs help. When you see this happening, here's how to respond.

Responding to an MWE Heart Attack

Restarting (CPR for the Mind, Will, and Emotions)

An MWE heart attack (prefrontal cortex overload) can be intense or relatively mild. Most often a major heart attack is preceded by many warning signs and symptoms. This is similar to a medical heart attack. The American Heart Association says this about heart attacks: *"Some heart attacks are sudden and intense — the 'movie heart attack,' where no one doubts what's happening. But most heart attacks start slowly, with mild pain or discomfort. Often people affected aren't sure what's wrong and wait too long before getting help."* MWE heart attacks are no different. Huge emotional blowups are almost always preceded by numerous small ones which go ignored.

This next tool is designed to be most effective in dealing with the symptoms of an oncoming MWE heart attack. When used in conjunction with the breaking agreements tool, your risk of suffering a major MWE Heart Attack is greatly reduced.

HERE ARE THE STEPS:

Start by regaining control of your breath.

You may not have realized it, but most likely your breathing has already been incrementally moving toward a panic breath pattern. It's possible you have been panic breathing for days without realizing it.

Breathe in deeply through your nose for a count of four. Count slowly: 1... 2... 3... 4.

Breathe out in the same way: 1... 2... 3... 4.

Now take your fingers and press on your forehead just above both of your eyebrows, about midway between the brow and the hairline. Keep the skin on your forehead taut as you press. We don't want to pinch. We want gentle, even pressure to stimulate the nerves in this area. This will in turn stimulate the prefrontal cortex.

As you are pressing, continue to count out your breaths. Adding one second to your outward breath each time or until you reach a point of discomfort.

In: 1... 2... 3... 4 and Out: 1... 2... 3... 4... 5

As you breathe, bring to mind the stressful thought, past, present, or future.

In: 1... 2... 3... 4 and Out: 1... 2... 3... 4... 5... 6

Continue breathing as the stress dissipates and is replaced by an awareness of your present self.

In: 1... 2... 3... 4... Out: 1... 2... 3... 4... 5... 6... 7

Think about the way the air feels as it moves through your body. Wiggle your toes and feel the texture of whatever is around them. Run your fingers across the fingers of your other hand and only pay attention to the feeling in the hand that is moving. (These things will stimulate the executive control centers of your brain.)

In: 1... 2... 3... 4... Out: 1... 2... 3... 4... 5... 6... 7... 8

Continue breathing intentionally until you feel ready to move on. You should be able to think more clearly and objectively now.

Repeat this restart process as necessary, anytime you feel yourself being overwhelmed with worry, fear, or anger.

"MWE Cardio" Long Term Prefrontal Health

- **Jump To Detox**

Right after using the restart tool is a great time to follow up using the "Breaking Agreements" tool described in the "Detoxify" section. Doing these together will strengthen the capacity of the neural network that deals with the issues you find overwhelming.

Start the breaking agreement tool by asking, "When was the first time I learned to feel anxious about (stressful thought)?" A memory will pop up and you can begin the process. (Hint: Go with the first memory even if you think it's unrelated.)

Say the memory out loud, so that you can hear it yourself with fresh ears.

Now ask:

Is there anyone I need to forgive? (Walk through the forgiveness steps.)

What lies did I begin to believe?

Did I make any vows in this memory?

Did I make or accept any judgments?

Listen quietly for a moment, and go with the first answer that comes to mind. Remember, you are reporting and not editing the thoughts that come to the screen. Even if it doesn't sound like something you currently believe, recall that we didn't ask about what you currently think you believe. We asked about what the you in the memory started to believe at that time.

Now, say the (lie, vow, judgment, or contract) out loud. Then:

"I break agreement with the (lie, vow, judgment, or contract.) that_____(repeat the specific lie, vow, judgment, or contract). That was not true."

See it in your hands, hold it out and say, "I do not want to carry this anymore, will you come and take this?"

(You may or may not see someone there, but the thing in your hand will disappear in some way.)

Ask, "What can I replace that with?"

Wait for something good to come and fill up the space that the infection once occupied. Be sure to figure out what it is replacing the infection, and lastly, how you plan on responding the next time you feel that way.

- **Appreciation Exercise**

You can strengthen your MWE cardio by making this next exercise a daily practice. This appreciation exercise will stimulate and strengthen the core areas of your emotional capacity.

There's a saying in the neurology world, "Neurons that fire together, wire together." Areas that frequently activate at the same time will develop a tangible wiring system that connects them. Think of it like the difference between winking and blinking. Because the eyes are neurologically linked together, blinking means that both eyes will close at the same time. Winking however, requires intentional control.

By intentionally activating areas of the brain together, you can help yourself create synaptic connections that neurologically link the thoughts together. This will cause a natural response of firing together, like blinking.

Doughnuts... Sweaters. Boom, we just made a weak little synaptic link. Don't worry it shouldn't last too long, but now, for a short while, anytime you hear "doughnuts" you will also think of sweaters. If you were to continually think of doughnuts and sweaters together, especially if you bonded them together with a good laugh, well then they might never come apart.

The Appreciation Exercise activates your mimetic network, the brain areas that give you your relational identity. At the same time it activates various places in your brain that contain the things you value and those that bring you happiness. By firing these areas together on a regular basis, they begin to fuse together. The way this exercise is done will cause you to release large quantities of dopamine. Dopamine is a happy feeling that functions like steroids in the brain. In fact, studies have shown that during infancy most of our brain development is attributed to dopamine. By linking our relational identity with value and joy, we can exponentially increase our ability to think clearly. We can also avoid going to T-Rex mode when our lives are not in danger.

HERE ARE THE STEPS:

1. *Start by picking someone. This can be literally anyone.*

2. *Think of some thing(s) you appreciate about them. This can be based on previous knowledge or casual observation. The less superficial the qualities you think of, the better.* (This engages your value and joy producers.)

3. *Make eye contact with them.* (This engages your mimetic identity network.)

4. *Smile. (This opens the flood of dopamine.)*

5. *Say to the person, "I like* _____*."* *(Fill in the blank with something you appreciate about them. e.g. "I like the way you carry yourself, so happy and confident.")*

6. *That's it, you're done! Can you feel that burst? Your brain is in heaven. You might even feel a little dizzy when you think of a really good one!*

Now, like some kind of highlander, you have acquired their powers. Don't worry; they will not be harmed. In fact, they have also become more powerful. It's a Win-Win.

Do this as often as possible with as many people as possible. You can even do this with yourself in the mirror. *Doughnuts.*

MWE Respiratory Failure

Recognizing MWE Respiratory Failure

If our social/emotional identity is the heart of our personality, then our expectations are the lungs of our personality. Our expectations, and the realization of those expectations, stimulate the release of dopamine. This is one of many chemical reactions that occur in our bodies based on how we feel. When we believe a situation calls for joy, we release dopamine throughout our body and brain. This stimulates the brain, increases brain activity in the frontal lobe (where our higher reasoning occurs), and it strengthens any active neurons involved in its release. In this way, dopamine functions in our personality much like oxygen functions in our body. This means that our ability to hope is the veritable lungs of who we are.

Interestingly, when we have hopeful thought or feeling, it is like we are experiencing joy in advance, this releases dopamine in our body too. Our social and emotional identity, higher level decision making, creativity, and problem solving all function better with the right amount of dopamine. This means that hope helps us to think clearly and make choices that reflect the value we have for our relationships and ourselves. Thus, hoping is like the act of drawing air into our personality.

A hope fulfilled is like life giving oxygen to our soul. When we get something we hoped for, pleasure and happiness (dopamine) floods the system and strengthens the neural pathways. This way you don't forget the mindset you were in when your hope was fulfilled. Conversely, when we don't get what we hoped for, our system to floods with glutamate which signals our brain to feel disappointment. The more glutamate, the more intensely we feel bummed out. This happens so that we don't forget which situations to avoid.

But, as life would have it, whenever glutamate is released, it comes mixed with an acid commonly known as "GABA." Think of GABA as a sort of neural painkiller. Interestingly, studies have shown that higher levels of serotonin, the neurological equivalent of contentment, can lessen the level of disappointment (glutamate) we experience without reducing the painkiller (GABA).

What does all this mean!? Let's put it all together. Hope is like breathing to your truest self. Your hope needs to match your brain activity like your breathing needs to match your physical activity. When this balance does not occur naturally, it is a sign of something unhealthy. If you tend to lose hope quickly, this would be similar to losing your breath quickly. If you feel overwhelmed by disappointments, if you are prone to shutting down, or if you find yourself short tempered when things don't go your way, these are all signs that your mental cardio system needs some exercise. Your hope breath isn't big enough to oxygenate your mind with dopamine. Be sure to use the "Appreciation Exercise" for a regular MWE cardio boost. There's also evidence to suggest that sitting quietly with someone who you feel fully accepts you can increase your levels of serotonin, which will then decrease the intensity of future disappointments.

When our hopes get dashed, the glutamate system designed to intensify disappointment encourages us to avoid the situation in the future. Unfortunately, many get the act of hoping mixed up with the situation itself. They stop breathing (hoping) altogether in an effort to avoid future pain. This is the equivalent of respiratory failure. This person needs intervention.

Responding to MWE Respiratory Failure

Eye to Eye Hope Resuscitation

Hope issues, though manageable, can often lead to more serious and life changing crisis. Have you ever heard the phrases, "drowning in problems," "choking on pride," "completely shut down," or "paralyzed by fear"? These all describe the same condition: someone who's true personality has stopped breathing-- they are losing all hope.

Many emotional drownings and hope blockages are preventable. A person with poor mental cardio health trying to survive an onslaught of problems is much more likely to "lose it." Someone in this state of depressive detachment needs immediate resuscitation. They can't get their own hope. They need you to give them yours. There is a powerful tool, that like mouth to mouth resuscitation, albeit intimate, can bring a person's true identity back to life. We call this tool "Eye to Eye Hope Resuscitation."

HERE ARE THE STEPS:

Start with eye contact. You want to maintain this throughout the entire process. Eye contact will engage the mimetic and social/emotional neural networks.

The left eye specifically has stronger neural pathways to the part of the brain that hosts our self-identity.

The right eye has stronger neural connection to the part of the brain which is most active when we feel happy and pleasant.

You can proceed using right or left eye contact indifferently or intentionally. Some prefer to feel it out and just stick with what feels natural and connected. Others will feel more effective by looking in the left eye when they are speaking about the personality and looking in the right eye when they are speaking about emotion.

Once eye contact is established, you will say the person's name with conviction. You want to grab the attention of the very core of their being. If they know what you're up to, you can say, "I am speaking to the you that is you." or "I want your spirit to come to attention." (This step lights up the right side prefrontal cortex, which has been observed in fMRI to be active during activities described as "profound" and "spiritual". This area is the only one even speculated to host our connection to consciousness.)

"Person's Name, I want you to listen."

Tell them three good things you know about them. (If this is not someone you know very well make some good guesses and leave out the "I know this because_____" part. You'll be surprised how accurate your guesses will be.)

"You are_____. I know this because_____."

"You are_____. I know this because_____."

"You are_____. I know this because_____."

Tell them three good things you hope for them.

"I hope that you_____."

"I hope that you_____."

"I hope that you_____."

This will be a powerful experience for both of you and best of all it can be implemented somewhat casually, even in the midst of a crisis.

You can wing it and speak from the heart or you can write down what you intend to say beforehand. Do not read it to the other person. This would negate the genuine connection you felt when writing it and compromise the intentional eye contact.

Do this in the mirror and your true personality will begin to flourish.

MWE Brokenness

Recognizing MWE Brokenness

At the core of our physical bodies, we have bones filled with marrow which produce our blood cells and give them the DNA that shapes us. This deepest place in us is protected by hard bones, tissue and skin. At the core of our personality, we have a will: a driving force that activates thought and identity, and is ultimately driven by the singular desire to live. Our will is the marrow of our soul. It is protected by our resolve to be who we are, which is both covered and animated by the muscles of our actions, and the skin of our social interactions. Our resolve to be ourselves is that hard bone protecting the will.

With enough trauma, the bones of our resolve can be broken. When that happens, our personality, at its core, fractures. The animation of our will and expressing our true selves can become so excruciating that everything in us begins to serve the sole function of protecting the broken place. The level of fracturing that can happen in a person ranges from very light, like a hairline fracture, to extremely shattered. Like our physical body, the severity of a personality fracture usually depends on: how hard we were hit with something, how heavy it was, and how big it was.

When a fracture happens, our core identity loses stability and cohesion. The extent of that instability will depend on the severity of the fracture. The most prominent symptom is that we no longer feel like one person. This occurs on a spectrum, but for the sake of simplicity, let's define it on three levels.

- **Hairline Fracture**

A hairline fracture happens when trauma goes through the skin of your social personality, through the muscle of your internal personality, and strikes the very bone of who you are, to the point that you begin to question your desire to be you. When this happens, the pain of keeping this part of you moving and participating in life is too much. This deep place in your identity is immobilized while every fiber of your ego swells around it to keep it safe. It feels as though the real you retreats into a hidden place while other parts of your personality--protectors and pretenders--come forward to participate in life for you and keep your emotional being safe. This is similar to the body's natural mechanism of swelling. The severity of a hairline fracture is comparatively minimal. Its symptoms are constant and feel like an internal argument with yourself. Often, as with any kind of fracture, you will experience unusual difficulty in making decisions.

- **Clean Break**

A clean break is higher on the the severity scale. It shares all of the same symptoms as a hairline fracture, but one. The main difference is the prominence of instability and separation in your identity. In a clean break, what was once one core skeleton of personality has separated into at least two parts. On top of painful, this feels very strange. You now seem to have another person inside of you telling you how to do life. Like trying to move a leg with a cleanly broken bone, any attempt to control this limb of your life will not only bring pain, but very strange behavior as well. In a clean break, you will have multiple inner voices until the bones can be reset and fused back together. This will require some professional help.

- **Shattered**

A shattered personality is usually due to having experienced severe trauma in repetition. In addition to all of the above symptoms, a shattered personality structure will feel like having many personalities without much semblance of reference to each other. A person with this type of wounding will likely lose time and do things they don't remember doing. Trying to figure out which pieces of personality go where is not going to work. Shattered bones require careful examination and care.

Responding to MWE Brokenness

If you have a shattered identity, getting on with life is not going to happen without help, but you can be put back together. If you feel you have a shattered identity, I highly recommend seeking out a program called "Heart Sync" by Dr. Andrew Miller. I also highly recommend "Shabar," developed by The Transformation Center in Redding, CA. Shabar is now available in many cities. These programs can help you determine the level of care you need and possibly guide you to the help of a counselor who specializes in Dissociative Identity Disorder (DID).

If you recognize this kind of brokenness in someone you know, your best course of action is to provide a splint by supporting and loving each part of them equally. Remind every part of them that they are cared for equally. Remember that while they may seem to be more than one person, they are actually one person broken into pieces. What we hope for them is that eventually those pieces come back together.

As in the physical body, it is a bad idea to aggravate a broken bone without knowing what's going on inside. For any personality brokenness that goes beyond a hairline fracture, let a specialist have a look at it and do your best to keep a stable environment around you. The people around you need to understand that you have an injury, that it is not permanent, that you are healing, and that until you are feeling better you will not be able to interact with them the way you normally would.

Treating minor fractures can be done at home with some caution and guidance. The moment things seem to become strained, painful, or convoluted, stop what you're doing. Take some rest and then consider asking someone with training in this area for help.

These steps can be very useful in discovering what's going on inside and possibly bring healing. Remember that this is an extremely simplified version of what could become a complex operation. If it doesn't seem to be working, there may be a more complex issue that needs to be addressed in a clinical setting. **I do not recommend attempting to lead anyone else through these steps. These are here if you want to try them for yourself. Read through all the steps before you begin.**

HERE ARE THE STEPS:

Go to a safe, quiet place.

Start by creating a clean empty space in your mind's eye.

Once you see or sense yourself in that space you can begin.

Ask, out loud, "When did my personality fracture?"

One of two things will happen. You will either see a memory of something traumatic or you will see nothing.

If you see nothing, it's for one of three reasons.

1. You are not ready to see it. If you're not ready, then you're not ready. A professional can help you get ready, if you desire help.

2. It could be that you have no fractures in your personality or …

3. You need to calm your mind. (Refer to the C-the memory steps for help focusing.)

If you see a memory, know that there may or may not be a fracture in it. Look around the memory as an observer.

Do you see yourself in the memory? (There may be more than one of you there. There may be young child versions of you hiding in the memory, so be sure to look for them.)

If you see yourself in the memory, ask yourself, "Are you stuck here?" You may or may not get an answer. Don't worry if you don't get one. Usually, you can feel if a part of you is stuck in the memory.

Once you have a good feel for any part or parts of you stuck in this memory, invite truth, as a person, to come into the memory. "Truth, I invite you into this memory. Come in to this place so I can see you here."

If you see truth enter into the memory, notice any changes or effects that truth has on the memory. It should feel lighter and more free.

Ask truth to lead the parts of you out of the memory and to take them to a safe place with him. "Truth will you please lead this part of me out of this memory and take him/her to a safe place?"

Address any reservations that the parts of you may express by redirecting their questions to truth. For instance, a part says, "I'm scared and I don't want to go." You say, "Truth, this part of me is scared and doesn't want to go. What do you want this part of me to know?"

If you get stuck at any point, you can try using the forgiveness and detox steps to loosen trauma from the memory. Stored trauma is what holds us captive to the past. Therefore sometimes before we can restore a fractured part, we must get it unstuck by releasing the trauma of the event.

If things get strange or painful, stop what you are doing and use the "Restart Tool" to cool any anxiety you are working up. Consider if you would like the help of a trained person to finish what you started or if you feel confident that you can continue on your own. Either way, be kind to yourself. Go at your own pace.

Once every part in the memory has walked out with truth, ask truth to release peace into the memory.

Look around and see how the memory has changed.

Ask truth to take you out of the memory and into a safe place too.

Describe the safe place that you see as it comes to you. Listen to your description of the place. As you do, more will come.

Ask truth to tell you more about this place.

Ask truth if you can meet him here later and at anytime you want.

Take your time with each step and do them carefully. Reading through this list of steps quickly with out engaging will do absolutely nothing for you. Repeat the process for as many memories that you feel may be holding a part of your personality in a state of distress and trauma.

Conclusion

Take these ideas; run with them. My hope is that by providing you with a good structure, you will get a feel for how to make these ideas your own. I want you to eventually pull the tools out of the structure I originally put them in and become proficient at using them freely. First Aid began when people with medical knowledge empowered the public to understand and own the power to heal that they, as trained professionals, possessed. The public didn't need to know everything. We just needed to know how to save a life. Once the public began to understand medical treatments, the medical field exploded into a renaissance of advancement. My hope is that you will take this knowledge and do what needs to be done to reconnect humanity with life. Globally, mankind is becoming more and more aware of the importance of our internal world. We can choose to manage our inner world well or we can let that world manage us. One is inevitable.

Epilogue

Our Connection To Life

To truly relate to ourselves and others in a healthy way I believe that we must come to terms with what I would call the trauma of our own existence. No matter how many "why" questions we answer to alleviate trauma, without a healthy connection to life we will live daily with the emptiness of belief in our own cosmic orphanhood. To exist without explanation is a trauma of it's own right. But when we truly consider what we are and how amazing our existence is, connection to life becomes inevitable.

In the universe, we observe what we call objects and forces. The objects are atomic elements that make stars, planets, and other celestial bodies. Then there are invisible forces causing those elements to react in certain ways. For example, imagine a giant cloud of random elements floating in space without gravity acting on them. Turn on the force of gravity, and suddenly those elements will begin to stick to each other based on their atomic weight and their relative distance to each other. Eventually that random cloud of elements will become stars, planets, and other celestial bodies. The force of gravity created a type of order out of disorder. (Stay with me here, this is coming to an important point.)

Gravity is only one of the many forces in the universe that creates order out of disorder. There are other forces such as the force that causes energy to solidify into a range of elements with varying properties, or the force that causes life to arise out of those elements. These invisible forces cause energy to exist. These energies under the influence of invisible forces cause elements. Finally, elements under the influence of energy and force cause life to arise. Ultimately everything is an expression of that invisible force, understood only in facets, such as gravity and the laws of energy. The more these forces interact with the objects and energies that they themselves have manifested, the greater the amount of order and complexity of order we observe.

Life as the Driving Force of Personality

Human beings are the most advanced expression of this order that we have seen in our universe. We are the most advanced exhibition of the nature of the force that we call life. This is why the very core of our personality is the drive not only to live, but to propagate life. The unspoken mission of humanity is to further the interests of life. Even in seemingly selfish survival situations when that nature of life wells up inside of us to fulfill our own needs and protect our own life, it does so because planted deep in us there is a voice of truth that says, "You are valuable. You must continue to live."

Upon a holistic examination, we must conclude that though this desire can be ferocious, its ferocity is not selfish. It is the ferocity of life. Life that is demanding to live. We have seen that when push comes to shove, our instinct is not solely selfish, but in fact it can become utterly selfless. We see this when parents, soldiers, and friends lay down their lives for the sake of others. The reality of self sacrifice is the full demonstration of the ultimate expression of man's ferocious determination to further the order of the universe. That, I believe is the fundamental nature of life. That, I believe is the true nature of man.

The very nature of our neurological design connects happiness to a thriving life and unpleasant feelings with the destruction of life. The simplest definition of dysfunction is when we confuse destructive habits for life giving ones. Deep down we do what we do because somewhere along the way we accepted the belief that what we are doing is in the interest of life. Good or bad, every decision we make is made in the interest of life as a whole, even in the counterintuitive circumstances in which people kill others. The logic will always lead you back to the progress of life as a whole.

That thought may give you pause. Aren't there evil people who just want to watch the world burn, who just want to punish and destroy lives? The answer is yes, but the real question is: why? It's a reflective judgment about our ability as humans to display the nature of life. Those who want to burn it all down have projected their own issues onto the world. Through their lenses they see that the world does not represent the nature of life, and then, for that reason, they decide it should no longer exist. Perhaps by their logic and experience we should be punished toward either change for the better or to our ultimate destruction. All logic leads back to life. The question is, will that life be heavenly, or will we choose to live in a hell of our own false perception?

I believe that the true purpose of our innermost will is to connect us to the force, energy, and progression of life. This means that mental health, in its purest essence, is the alignment of our identity with a true understanding of life, and realizing that life itself is the greater being of which we are all a part. If we clean up our wounds, we can heal. If we heal, we will be able to see past the pain. If we see past the pain, we will see life as it was meant to be seen. We will see ourselves and others with the hope of our greatest potential, living as benevolent expressions of beauty, order, and intelligence.

Redefining Our Relationship With Life

We do not have a subject-object relationship with the universe. We are not a thing that is separate from the planet we live on, nor the star we revolve around. Our bodies are the very same elements that once floated around in space. Those elements are now responding to a force in the universe that brings them into order and causes them to reflect that force. Your body absorbs photons from the sun every day. Those photons leave their mass energy in your body and become part of you. Your body is ever-changing with every bit of food that you eat. Every thought that you have, and every thing that you observe literally changes your physical brain. So, where does your body, mind, will, or emotion end and the rest of the universe begin?

95

We humans have become what we are because of an invisible force expressed in physical laws. A force that takes stardust and guides it into becoming a universe with living things in it. You are not your body and mind. Your body and mind are an ever changing river of atoms coming and going, flowing around an invisible force of nature shaped like you. You are your particular expression of the force of life itself. This is the unavoidable paradox we have come to by studying the physical universe: we are indelibly connected with forces that we cannot clearly define. No matter how scientific I try to keep my words, the journey will ultimately become existential. It would seem that all streams of inquiry do lead to one inevitable indescribable ocean.

I have done my best to leave these undefinable experiences undefined. Like an impressionist, I want to leave you with the responsibility of discovering the meaning for yourself. We interact with what we call "truth,". We interact with what we call "life,". We probe what we assume is our subconscious. We speculate about our deepest person, and we might also pray to God with the very same mode, mind, and method. I do not see the edges, I do not see the difference between these things and therefore I try not to paint them on the tools that I am handing you. Every road of certainty leads to uncertainty and every road of mystery leads to discovery.

Every time I describe interacting with what I have been calling the "voice of truth" or "the force of life," I do so from my own perspective and vantage point. As generic as I may feel those terms to be, others will insist that I have not captured the full picture. They are right! All we can do is embrace the mystery that we have access to an inner voice. A voice that speaks life to us. The discovery of what that means is a journey that we must experience in our relationships with each other, our relationship with ourselves, and our relationship with life. Take these tools and heal the wounds hindering your ability to live, to thrive, and to know love. As you do, things will become clearer, more vibrant, and full of meaning. Here's to a beautiful journey!

Recommended Reading and Source Materials

Much of this guide is the assimilation of many years of knowledge and experiences passed on to me by incredible, intelligent, and delightful people. Some of them have published materials which I have included in this list along with any books that have provided guidance and information that helped to shape First Aid MWE.

1. The Science of Mental Health, Vol. 10: Fear and Anxiety by Steven E. Hyman (Editor)

2. Vandals at the Gates of Medicine (1995) and Medical Warrior: Fighting Corporate Socialized Medicine (1997). Miguel A. Faria Jr., MD.

3. Lebreton et al. "Your Goal Is Mine: Unraveling Mimetic Desires in the Human Brain" The Journal of Neuroscience, 2012

4. The Puppet of Desire, Jean-Michel Oughourlian

5. Desire Found Me, Andre Rabe

6. Origins of the Modern Mind: Three Stages in the Evolution of Culture, Merlin Donald

7. "The Biology of Joy" Article by Michael D. Lemonick, http://charterforcompassion.org/node/4349

8. Evolve Your Brain: The Science of Changing Your Mind, Joe Dispenza

9. Joy Starts Here, E. James Wilder, Ed M. Khouri, Chris M. Coursey, and Shelia D. Sutton

10. 101 Trauma-Informed Interventions: Activities, Exercises and Assignments to Move the Client and Therapy Forward, By Linda A. Curran, BCPC, LPC, CACD, CCDPD, EMDR Level II Trained

11. (Not So Great) Expectations: Expectations: use them or be used by them, David Rock https://www.psychologytoday.com/blog/your-brain-work/200911/not-so-great-expectation, Posted Nov 23, 2015

12. Feeling Bummed? How Disappointment Works in the Brain, Christopher Wanjek http://www.livescience.com/48022-disappointment-brain.html

13. The Brain, Top to Bottom, Bruno Dubuc, http://thebrain.mcgill.ca

14. Warning Signs of A Heart Attack, American Heart Association. http://www.heart.org/ HEARTORG/Conditions/HeartAttack/WarningSignsofaHeartAttack/Warning-Signs-of-a-Heart-Attack_UCM_002039_Article.jsp

15. Freedom Tools, Andy Reese

16. The Effects of Trauma and How to Deal With It, Jim Banks

17. Who Switched Off My Brain, Dr. Caroline Leaf

18. Understanding the Mysteries of Human Behavior, Professor Mark Leary, Duke University

www.ingramcontent.com/pod-product-compliance
Lightning Source LLC
Chambersburg PA
CBHW060130050426
42448CB00010B/2055